SPIRITUAL KRYPTONITE

The Battle against Lust

Satan might have won the battle but he won't win the War.

This is a Warfare Devotional outlining the Biblical Facts of Recovery. Welcome to the Spiritual Bootcamp Workbook.

Authored by: Pastor Carl Flowers

Trinity Outreach Publishing
502 Jarrell St
Picayune, MS 39466

For information address Trinity Outreach Publishing Rights Department, 502 Jarrell St, Picayune, MS 39466

First Paperback edition December 2016

Manufactured in the United States of America

ISBN-13:
978-0692816110 (Carl Flowers)

ISBN-10:
0692816119

It is my prayer that this will be made available to Christian bookstores and distributors worldwide.
This book may be used for the teaching and counseling of Men's Ministries, Women's Ministries, Singles Ministries, and Addiction Ministries. It is a workbook designed to equip people who struggle with any addiction.

DEDICATION

To the most caring and wonderful woman in the world, my precious wife, Julie for her increasing Love and commitment to me, our Family, and the kingdom of God.

To my son, Justin, to my Daughter Tayla, to my grandchildren, Ra'Nyra, Jaidyn, and Nova Flowers.

To my church family and staff at Trinity Outreach Ministries, who faithfully loved and supported me over the years.

To my Mother Joyce Mclaurin, who has faithfully labored, physically and prayerfully on my behalf.

To my Spiritual Father, Apostle Jimmy Peters and to all the leaders and Coaches who invested in my life.

To all the men and women who looked to me as a father & mentor; because of you, this book has come to fruition.

To my Lord and Savior, who has delivered and set me free, who has made all things possible for me.

I also dedicate this book to the "We Still Do Marriage: Ministry of Trinity Outreach Ministries. This book is a reminder of the Vows we have made onto the Lord.

This book is dedicated to anyone who ever struggled with any type of addiction. The contents is a collection of my sermons and Bible study notes that inspired me through over 23 years of deliverance. It is my prayer that this book be a tool to recovery in order to combat that spirit in the battle of lust. satan might have won the battle but he won't win the war .

The Battle is the Lord's

I Samuel 17:47 - AND ALL THIS ASSEMBLY SHALL KNOW THAT THE LORD SAVETH NOT WITH SWORD AND SPEAR; FOR THE BATTLE IS THE LORD'S, AND HE WILL GIVE YOU INTO OUR HANDS.

I pray that this book will be an inspiration to all Christians, as well as unbelievers.

Forward

It is so perfectly God ordained that Apostle Carl Flowers would title a book "Spiritual Kryptonite". From the first time I met Apostle Flowers, I immediately knew there was something very different about this man of God. He has a genuine humbleness before God and a quiet meekness & unconditional love about him that is very unique in today's me-first world. Apostle Flowers is a man of quiet peace, yet at the same time, he exudes Holy Spirit fire unlike I had ever experienced before meeting him. It is a strengthening power that comes from deep within him, from the very core of his being, a Faith in knowing Who God is and believing God can do and will do what He says He can and will do. That faith fueled God-given power is so strong that it overflows onto those around Carl Flowers and commands a reverence and respect for the great anointing that Almighty God has bestowed upon him. It is a power that literally demonstrates what Christ meant when He said "greater works shall you do", one that commands the enemy to flee, heals the sick, and raises the dead soul to new life everlasting in Christ.

Here, as in his two prior books, "From Sin & Shame to Glory" and "Finish Strong", as well as in his lectures, bible studies, and sermons, Apostle Carl Flowers uses what he knows to be Truth through the learning halls of his very own life, affirmed through his own battles & experiences, confirmed through his own testimony to bring us the same powerful "how-to" in overcoming the enemy.

Once Again, Apostle Flowers brings us his insatiable hunger for the Word of God, and his love of sharing in revelation knowledge in order to give generously to others the freedom in Christ and power of Holy Spirit that He has been so graciously given. I urge you dear reader to devour the God inspired pages of "Spiritual Kryptonite" so you too can learn how to draw closer to God, fight the good fight and battle to overcome the enemy as my dear Pastor, Mentor and Friend, Apostle Carl Flowers, shares here.

Lisa Daughdrill

Pastor and Co-Founder – Grace House Ministries
Co-Author of "My Name is Victory"
Picayune, MS

The most important thing is to be honest with yourself that there is a problem, because if you can't confess that there is an issue, then how can that issue be fixed? You must get to know and understand what your kryptonite is and what or who causes you to be vulnerable. You hear a lot of people blaming things on the devil but what about those self- inflecting things we cause on ourselves? After you work the 12 steps and be faithful to them only then can true deliverance come about. Do you want to be delivered from bondage so the guilt and shame can bring you to your glory and lead you to your destiny? I, like you and every born again believer, had to take control of my ear and eye gates. This is why we walk by faith and not by sight. We know that we all have fallen and come short of the glory of God but he's a just God. Take him at his word. He's a God that can't lie. I choose not to wear the mask or to hide my fears or the darkness that lies, but to be exposed to the light and truth of God. Remember, trouble doesn't always last and what the devil meant for bad God will work it for your good. Being a part of this

Trinity Outreach has changed my life forever. No matter where I go, I still have a place to call home. What I love the most about my Pastor and Elect Lady is they are livings testimonies. I have been deep down in sin, more like the prodigal son, but every time they saw me they called me daughter or Minster. They spoke life into me in every dead situation in my life so when people say wow to the songs God allows me to sing, just know I'm in the vein of my mother and father.

Minister Maria Johnson
Minister – Trinity Outreach Ministries
Picayune, MS

Spiritual Kryptonite has a way of creeping into your life at any given time. Even at my strongest point, I relapsed, also too at my weakest point. The word of God declares, "Put on the whole armor of God, that ye may be able to withstand the wiles of the devil".

As a child of God I wish I woke up fully armored every morning, but it doesn't work that way. Ephesians 6:11 said, "PUT ON THE WHOLE ARMOR OF GOD", which cautions me to put on my protection. There are points of vulnerability where Spiritual Kryptonite has its chance to blind side me if I haven't assembled the WHOLENESS of God's armor purposed for me. Once I have it on, I "MAY" be able to "Stand". Each piece of armor that I put on is battle tested. I won't know if it will "Stand" if it hasn't passed or failed the engagement of spiritual warfare in my life. The more in life I have fought through my personal addictions to include lust, drugs, sex, money, power, and fleshly behavior of this world, the more I learned that I need to be closer to God to acquire a more personalized armor that is especially made for me to stand. We are super natural beings who serve a far more superior God. The Kryptonite I'm speaking of had me at ground "0" where I lost it all and believed I was winning. This was a direct result of lack of intimacy with God. God has a way with circumventing the excess in our lives to afford us to see things from the best perspective. Gods will for ours live enables us to have life and have it more abundantly.

Minister Andre Johnson
Minister – Trinity Outreach Ministries
Picayune, MS

Apostle Carl Flowers has first-hand revelation knowledge in smashing the lies of the enemy through addiction recovery counseling and mentorship. As a former addict, recovered by the blood of Jesus poured upon me, I am grateful for a workbook such as Spiritual Kryptonite that will help thousands like me find true freedom in the One who saves and transforms. Honored and blessed are words that epitomize how I feel about knowing Apostle Carl Flowers, a man who I firmly believe is an angel sent directly from heaven for such a time as this.

I am in awe of his humility as he reaches thousands with the Gospel of Jesus Christ. Carl Flowers is a man who has been called to raise up Christian leaders, even those who have struggled against the enemy and seen the darkest days imaginable in their own lives, and show them the way to go and how to withstand the daily beatings of the enemy while fighting on the front lines of battles unseen.

I am forever grateful to know that I am not alone, and it is because of men of honor like this man of God that I am who I am today, for he walked this out ahead of me and was able to show me the way through his own story. Spiritual Kryptonite is a divine blessing from above that has the power to break strongholds and inspire those seeking a new life in freedom. The lessons taught in this book from a lifetime of experience are nuggets that will stand the test of time.

Julie Keene
Author of #JWGirl4Life – Where the Light Meets the Dark"
Author of Coming Full Circle Blog
Co-Author of "Just Susan – #BrandNewKindaFree"
Co-Author of "My Name is Victory"
Biloxi, MS

And He Himself gave some to be apostles, some prophets, some evangelists, and some pastors and teachers, for the equipping of the saints for the work of ministry…that we should no longer be children, tossed to and fro and carried about with every wind of doctrine, by the trickery of men, but speaking the truth in love…That you put off, concerning your former conduct, the old man which grows corrupt according to the deceitful lusts, and be renewed in the spirit of your mind, and that you put on the new man which was created according to God, in true righteousness and holiness. Ephesians 4:11, 14-15, 22-24

Apostle Carl Flowers has exercised in many gifts, to include each of those recorded above, since our first meeting. His gifts have continued to make room for him with his most recent being the authorship and publication of his third book. *Spiritual Kryptonite* is charged with powerful testimonies that are infused by the word of God and delivered right to the inner man of each of us. From "The Struggle is Real" to "Training the Eyes" to "Accountability", every single page is fabricated with the anointed God-sent truth. A truth that so many young marriages are starving for. A truth that single men and women of all ages can't live without.

As overseers of the "We Still Do" ministry at Trinity Outreach Ministries, we have seen first-hand what the enemy's plan is for the family. Unfortunately, lust is a fleshly gate that the enemy frequently enters through, causing insurmountable destruction to the core of what God did in Genesis when he made man a companion. From the outside looking in, some relationships may appear perfect. They almost seem invincible, like superman. BUT, there is no such thing as a perfect marriage. There will be struggles. Foxes, whether small or large come in and disrupt harmony.

The enemy knows our weaknesses and he uses them to cause strife and confusion. This takes a toll on any relationship; spreading and causing ties to be weakened. If not identified, and put in check, it will ultimately lead to destruction. The enemy is much like a radioactive substance to a relationship-- its kryptonite. And just as it effects superman, it effects man and woman. Apostle Carl Flowers wrote *Spiritual Kryptonite* to help each of us explore our weakness so that it may be identified and rebuked. Superman regained his strength from the sun; *Spiritual Kryptonite* is a guide to helps us regain our strength through the true and living Word of God.

It is our prayer, that every person who reads the pages of this book be overcome by the anointing that rests on each page. We pray that the examples and the scriptures will be written in your heart, and that a hedge of protection be placed around each of you so that the enemy may not devour the sound teachings. We also pray that the teachings will strengthen your relationship with Christ, and thereby, your relationship with both your inner man and your spouse.

We are honored to sit under such a blessed Man of God who has changed our lives forever through his unwavering obedience. He is a phenomenal example of humility and one who has shown himself approved through his study. Our faith has been strengthened under him...Our anointing has been poured under him...Our hearts have been restored under him...Our marriage has been made stronger under him...Our children have Christ in their hearts because of him...Our finances have grown under him. Our families have been saved under him. Our daughter has been healed from Bell's Palsy under him. He has impacted every area of our lives and we assure you that *Spiritual Kryptonite* will do the same for you. Apostle Carl Flowers' leadership is one that inspires transformation and delivers deliverance.

Mr. and Mrs. Demetrious and Bria Goff
Armor Bearer, We Still Do Ministry
Trinity Outreach Ministries

Introduction

The Glory of God's plan and the power of is spiritual weapons in our warfare' is that they work. We need to learn how to think and how to ask God for what will work for us personally to deliver us from bondage. All issues are dead issues and hinder us greatly if we don't seek God for total deliverance.

In this book, "Spiritual Kryptonite", you will discover 12 chapters, notes, bible study outlines, my sermon notes, and testimonies of deliverance for journaling your thoughts on your road to recovery. Enjoy the power packed lessons that God used to start me on the road to deliverance. The Holy Spirit inspired me to give the reader some nuggets to help start the recovery process from the chains of any addiction enjoy God will deliver you from Sin & Shame and bring you to the Glory. If you relapse in life, just get up and Finish Strong.

This is Book is an Arsenal of Deliverance for Deliverance

SPIRITUAL KRYPTONITE

Table of Contents

CHAPTER 1 - THE STRUGGLE IS REAL - THE PROBLEM WITH LUST

Congratulation you have taken the first step to a better and broader understanding of your spiritual battles! Thank you for your interest in this book. It is my prayer that as you read through the 12 chapters it will be an asset to you and your family, your friends, or anyone that you know struggles with an addiction. Spiritual Kryptonite is written to be a tool that will help the teacher as well as the students through the process of recovery. Growing up I was inspired by Superman, The Incredible Hulk, Batman, and Spider-Man. The defeated Superman was exposed to Kryptonite (which was Superman's weakness) and that inspired me to title this book "Spiritual Kryptonite". Of course, as you've read in my last two books, "From Sin & Shame to Glory" and "Finish Strong", I have been very transparent with my story of how God delivered me.

In my battles with the lust of drugs and alcohol addiction as well as pornography, the only exit I had out of it was to surrender my life to Jesus Christ. It is my prayer that this book will be a blessing to you. Again, I'm not writing as though I have arrived in perfection. I will confess the struggle is real and the only thing that is keeping me is the word of God. It is the only way to recover from any addiction, in every area of our lives. This book is meant to inspire you, as well as myself, to continue to walk in total submission to the word of God. I have a passion to help people and this book has been very therapeutic. It is a reminder to me of what God brought me from and the grace that he has on my life as well as the call. The Lord has great things for you. As you begin to go through these pages, each chapter will touch on every aspect of ministry dealing with men and women, marriages, singles ministry, and addiction recovery. Lust is a major problem and if we don't discover our spiritual weapons, we will be ultimately defeated in every area of our life. Most people don't understand the struggles of others and they look at you in a different way once they hear of your story, but I am not ashamed of the gospel of Christ. I would rather tell the story, embrace the glory, and show that I had been a victim to addictive behavior that had me bound. Our success is in our surrender. We have two choices: to come clean or stay away nasty. We might've done what the worlds says we've done, but we are not who the world says we are.

Superman possesses the powers of flight, superhuman strength, x-ray vision, heat vision, cold breath, super-speed, enhanced hearing, and nigh-invulnerability. While Superman is immensely strong, both in terms of muscle power and the ability to take physical punishment, he is not all-powerful.

Kryptonite is universally understood as a term describing a person's fundamental weakness. Kryptonite's effect on Superman varies between adaptations of the story, with some depicting Superman as merely weakened with his powers blocked and others showing him collapsing and completely unable to move. Either way, though, kryptonite gives the villain an easy advantage over Superman and if a villain understands how it works, he could strategically use its effects to defeat the man of steel. Although kryptonite essentially renders Superman useless, it's a driving reason behind why Superman is such a fantastic superhero and why his character is so successful. If Superman was invincible all the time, no villain would ever stand a chance again him, and he would simply be a boring stock character that never faces any real conflicts. With kryptonite, villains are able to gain the upper hand and make the drama of Superman's universe a worthwhile adventure.

The biblical story of Samson, a strongman whose secret lies in his uncut hair, and his love for Delilah, the woman who seduces him, discovers his secret, and then betrays him to the Philistines.

David's seduction of Bathsheba, told in 2 Samuel 11, is omitted in the Books of Chronicles. The story is that David, while walking on the roof of his palace, saw Bathsheba, who was then the wife of Uriah, having a bath. He immediately desired her and later made her pregnant.
In an effort to conceal his sin, and save Bathsheba from punishment for adultery, David summoned Uriah from the army (with whom he was on campaign) in the hope that Uriah would re-consummate his marriage and think that the child was his. Uriah was unwilling to violate the ancient kingdom rule applying to warriors in active service. Rather than go home to his own bed, he preferred to remain with the palace troops.
After repeated efforts to convince Uriah to have sex with Bathsheba, the king gave the order to his general, Joab, that Uriah should be placed on the front lines of the battle, where it was the most dangerous, and left to the hands of the enemy (where he was more likely to die). David had Uriah himself carry the message that ordered his death. After Uriah was dead, David made the now widowed Bathsheba his wife.

David's action was displeasing to the Lord, who accordingly sent Nathan the prophet to reprove the king.

After relating the parable of the rich man who took away the one little ewe lamb of his poor neighbor (2 Samuel 12:1-6), and exciting the king's anger against the unrighteous act, the prophet applied the case directly to David's action with regard to Bathsheba.

The king at once confessed his sin and expressed sincere repentance. Bathsheba's child by David was struck with a severe illness and died a few days after birth, which the king accepted as his punishment.

Every one of us has had something in their life that we yielded to that was not healthy for our spirit man whether it was drugs/alcohol, pornography, infidelity, over eating, or the like. It was a major problem. As a result, we had a lot of failures because of our spiritual weakness. Often times, if we don't discover what it is that really comes to steal our joy and will develop habits and dysfunctions of moral decay many people are struggling with different type of addictions.

Unfortunately the divorce rate is high and there are many single-parent homes. Infidelity, drug addiction, and numerous problems and weaknesses can be defined as spiritual Kryptonites. When we don't take full control of our spirit man by admitting that we have a problem, we fall into sin.

This is not to say that we are super Christians, super dad, supermom, are super children. This world has a lot of lust and ungodly soul ties that destroy families at an alarming rate. In order to overcome, we need to discover our spiritual weaknesses.

Lust is a major problem. If we don't learn how to train our eyes or pinpoint the source of the problem it will eventually destroy us. This book was written to help men in and women who have battled with the spirit of lust. Satan might have won the battle but he won't win the war.

The lust of the eye - pornography can destroy your family. As wonderful as the Internet is, it is also a Pornography Pipeline into your house! Just recently I read that today there are 200,000 people hooked on pornographic sites and X-rated chat rooms. The researchers said that "cybersex compulsives spent more than 11 hours a week at X-rated sites." There are now at least 400,000 sex-oriented sites on the World Wide Web. A national opinion poll found that 57% of Americans believed that pornography was the chief instigator of the "breakdown of morals, and the encouragement of the crime of rape."

In a survey of over 500 Christian men at a men's retreat, over 90% admitted that they were feeling disconnected from God because lust, porn, or fantasy had gained a foothold in their lives. As reported in an article on Pastors.com by Kenny Luck.

In March 2005, Christianity Today published the results of a study called "Christians and Sex" in their Leadership Journal. 680 pastors and 1,972 laypersons were surveyed, with the following results:

1. 44% of churchgoers want to hear more scriptural teaching from their pastors on the subject of sex.
2. 22% of pastors feel they should spend more time on the topic.

3. 85% of pastors say they speak about sexual issues once a year, while 63% of churchgoers say their pastors do so. Among those churchgoers who say they want their pastors to preach more about sexual issues, 47% say their pastor speaks about it once a year, an even bigger difference of opinion. A CTI analyst was quoted saying "Perhaps this desire for more biblical exposition on sexual issues exists because pastors are not speaking forcefully or clearly enough, while exposure to sexual images and messages in today's media is ever more heightened."

4. 57% of pastors say that addiction to pornography is the most sexually damaging issue to their congregation.

5. Almost 9 in 10 pastors reported counseling a layperson on sexual issues once a year or more.

We hear and read about that statistics. It is time to educate ourselves by equipping ourselves through the Word of God. There is hope for anyone. Do not allow your weakness to destroy you. Learn how to guard your heart and train your eyes. Use the Word of God as your spiritual weapon to defeat your spiritual strongholds. This book is basic training. The Word is God is our code of conduct.

How can we win the war against lust and the overt sexual sin which results from lust?

_____

_____

_____

_____

_____

_____

_____

_____

_____

_____

We're bombarded daily with sensuality. You can't watch TV, read a news magazine or drive past bill boards without being confronted with blatantly sexual pictures and messages. We all know that as Christians, we are to avoid sexual immorality.

The tough question is, How?

List your struggles of Defeat:

_____
_____
_____
_____
_____
_____
_____
_____
_____
_____

How has your struggle affected you personally?

_____
_____
_____
_____
_____
_____
_____
_____
_____

How has it affected your family?

_____

_____

_____

_____

_____

_____

_____

_____

_____

_____

_____

List your accomplishments of victory:

_____

_____

_____

_____

_____

_____

_____

_____

_____

_____

What is the most recent battles you have won dealing with your addictions?

_____

_____

_____

_____

_____

_____

_____

_____

_____

_____

1. What do I enjoy about my addiction, what does it do for me (be specific)?

_____
_____
_____
_____
_____
_____
_____
_____
_____
_____
_____

List as many things as you can that you liked about whatever you are/were addicted to.

- Where possible, find alternative ways of achieving the same goals.
- Recognize positive thinking about the addiction as a potential relapse warning sign.
- Realize that there are some things you liked about the addiction you will have to learn to live without.
- List what you enjoy about your addiction so you can ask yourself if it is really worth the price.
- Realize that you aren't stupid; you did get something from your addiction. It just may not be working on your behalf anymore.

_____
_____
_____
_____
_____
_____
_____
_____
_____
_____

2. What do I hate about my addiction; what bad things does it do to me and to others (give specific examples)?

_____
_____
_____
_____
_____
_____
_____
_____
_____
_____

List as many of the bad, undesirable results of your addiction as you can. Here it is extremely important that you use specific examples. Specific examples have much greater emotional impact and motivational force!

- Ask yourself honestly "If my addiction was a used car, would I pay this much for it? If you wouldn't pay this much for it, why not?
- Review this list often, especially if you are having a lot of positive,
  happy thoughts about all the great things your addiction did for you and how much fun you had in pursuing it.

_____
_____
_____
_____
_____
_____
_____
_____
_____

3. What do I think I will like about giving up my addiction?

_____

_____

_____

_____

_____

_____

_____

_____

_____

_____

List what good things you think about or fantasize will happen when you stop your addiction.

- This provides you with a list of goals to achieve and things to look forward to as a result of your new addiction free lifestyle.
- This list also helps you to reality test your expectations. If they are unrealistic, they can contribute to relapse based on disappointment, depression, or self-pity.

_____

_____

_____

_____

_____

_____

_____

_____

4. What do I think I won't like about giving up my addiction?

_____

_____

_____

_____

_____

_____

_____

_____

_____

List what you think you are going to hate, dread
or merely dislike about living without your
addiction.

- This list tells you what kinds of new coping
  skills, behaviors and lifestyle changes you
  need to develop in order to stay addiction
  free.
- It also serves as another relapse warning list.
  If all you think about is how much life
  sucks now that you are not in active
  addiction, you are engaging in a relapse
  thought pattern that is just as dangerous by
  only focusing on what you liked about your
  addiction.

_____

_____

_____

_____

_____

_____

_____

_____

_____

This is not a do once and forget about it exercise.
It is an ongoing project. Most people simply can't
remember all of the positive and negative aspects
of addiction and recovery at any one time.
Furthermore, seeing all the negative consequences
of addiction listed in one place is very powerful.
On the positive side, most people do not
absolutely know for certain what they will like or
will not like about living free of their addictions
until they have done so for some time. I know of
people who continued to add items to all four
questions for a full 6 months.

Journal your thoughts:

_____

_____

_____

_____

_____

_____

_____

_____

_____

_____

_____

_____

_____

_____

_____

_____

_____

_____

_____

_____

_____

_____

_____

_____

_____

_____

_____

_____

_____

_____

_____

_____

_____

_____

BREAKOUT SESSION

Spiritual Weapons Against Lust

We need to clearly understand the will of God.

1 Thessalonians 4:2-5 - For you know what commandments we gave you through the Lord Jesus. For this is the will of God, your sanctification: that you should abstain from sexual immorality; that each of you should know how to possess his own vessel in sanctification and honor, not in passion of lust, like the Gentiles who do not know God.

Challenge: Do "you know"? You must know the precise "will of God" if you hope to achieve it. His will for us is our "sanctification" — the continuing work of God in us that makes us more like Christ. This requires knowing how to go forward without living "in passion of lust."

_____

_____

_____

_____

_____

_____

_____

_____

_____

_____

_____

_____

_____

_____

_____

_____

_____

_____

_____

_____

CHAPTER 2 - REMEMBER THE BATTLE PLAN

1. No temptation lasts forever. They may feel like they will, but eventually they will fade.

Journal your thoughts:

_____

_____

_____

_____

_____

_____

_____

_____

_____

_____

2. Perseverance will often be your most important asset. When the waves of lust would start to roll over me, I would offer up one or two weak prayers, the battle would get harder, and I would give in. I've waged battles with lust that lasted all night, sleeping for an hour, getting hit, praying and resisting, falling asleep for another hour or two, and then repeating the cycle. You've got to be prepared to go the distance, no matter how long it takes.

Journal your thoughts:

_____

_____

_____

_____

_____

_____

_____

3. You have every weapon you need to stand firm in the battle. I now know that prayer and God's Word are enough to overcome every battle. I didn't always believe this. When lust had a foothold in my life, God's Word and prayer didn't seem to have any power for me. I used a combination of white knuckling my way through temptation (which didn't work), or calling a friend and asking them to pray for me (which worked for an hour or two, but when the lust attack hit again I still needed a way to stand on my own). This does not mean that we shouldn't try to fight lust in isolation or on our own strength, but that there will always be times in our life when we can't get a friend on the phone, or get to a group, and we must stand our ground. In those moments we need to be able to wield the weapons God has given every believer. My problem in the past was that I had lost so many battles after reading the Bible or praying that I didn't believe either of these had the power to see me through. Prayer is powerful; it connects me with the Lord and His power and brings in the emotional and spiritual firepower I need to press through to victory. God's Word is a sword that cuts to the core of my flesh, which would love to indulge in lust, if I let it. The battle may be fierce, and it could go on for a while, but eventually the power of prayer and His word are enough to take me through.

Journal your thoughts:

_____
_____
_____
_____
_____
_____
_____
_____
_____
_____
_____

4. In war, one side will eventually get worn down and give up. You never have to be the side that surrenders.

Journal your thoughts:

_____
_____
_____
_____
_____
_____
_____
_____
_____
_____

5. What you believe will play a critical factor in determining the outcome. If you believe that you've fallen too many times to overcome lust, or that your flesh and the enemy are too powerful, you're already halfway to defeat. I've had plenty of men tell me over the years that they had little to no hope that they could ever be set free from lust. If you believe that victory is possible, not by fighting with your willpower or flesh, which won't work, but with the tools God

has given you, then there is more than
enough hope that you will come through.

Journal your thoughts:

_____
_____
_____
_____
_____
_____
_____
_____
_____
_____

6. Like Joseph with Potiphar's wife, there will
   be some battles where the sexual energy is
   too strong and delaying is dangerous; the
   only way to win is to run, immediately. For
   example, if a woman who was not your wife
   was touching you or asking you to sleep
   with her, excuse yourself and get out of
   there. Stay away; don't play with fire.

Journal your thoughts:

_____
_____
_____
_____
_____
_____
_____
_____
_____
_____

7. Use wisdom and discernment regarding
   your weak points. If there is a situation
   you've placed yourself in many times and

have fallen, avoid it. Don't play games with
lust.

Journal your thoughts:

_____
_____
_____
_____
_____
_____
_____
_____
_____
_____

8. Examine what you really believe about
    yourself, God, and lust. Is He really strong
    enough to see you through? Does He even
    care? Do you believe He hears your cries for
    help?

Journal your thoughts:

_____
_____
_____
_____
_____
_____
_____
_____
_____
_____

9. Remember who you are. You are God's son
    (or daughter, as women struggle with lust
    too). You are not alone and you are not
    forsaken. He is near (Philippians 4). If
    you're married and have kids, remember
    that you are your wife's husband and your

children's father. Think about how it will feel if you have to look your wife/husband in the eye and tell her/him the shame of your Lust. Remember your children and the shame you will feel knowing you're not the man/woman they think you are, should you fall. Be who are you are, a blood-bought, son or daughter of the living God, with loved ones who need you to be the leader of their home.

Journal your thoughts:

_____
_____
_____
_____
_____
_____
_____
_____
_____
_____

10. Remember that just because you've failed in the past does not mean you have to fall again. You don't have to give in! The battle may be intense, but if you learn to lean on God and use the tools He's given you, you'll start chalking up some wins.

Journal your thoughts:

_____
_____
_____
_____
_____
_____
_____
_____

_____

_____

11. You are not a loser, or a failure. You are broken, weak and struggle with a flesh that screams for lust, but you're not the scum the enemy has been trying to tell you that you are. Beating yourself up is playing into the enemy's hands because it keeps you in "I don't deserve freedom and victory" mode. Accept God's forgiveness for your past sins once and for all. It's done. Move forward and keep going.

Journal your thoughts:

_____
_____
_____
_____
_____
_____
_____
_____
_____
_____

12. You have more spiritual firepower than you realize. The enemy wants to keep you in the dark about this. Every prayer, every time you read Scripture aloud, is an assault against him and your flesh. He doesn't like getting hit, and if you continue to persevere eventually you'll be the one wearing him down.

Journal your thoughts:

_____
_____
_____
_____
_____

_____
_____
_____
_____
_____
_____

13. In every battle, in order to win, you must choose to allow your flesh to die. You don't fight against your flesh with willpower, but you ignore its cries to indulge in sin. You let it die. There will be a little pain inside; I notice that when I let my flesh die that there's a momentary intensifying of the craving for lust, then a strong feeling like I've lost or missed out on something. Not long after, it's over. My flesh has died, and along with it the lust-craving. If you pray and read God's Word but you're not willing to die, you will eventually lose the battle because your flesh will take over. There are times when my only prayer during temptation is "God, please help me to die." I know what's really going on is that my flesh is craving sin and I have to die; it's not about the enemy, it's just that there's this sin-thing inside of me that wants to go the wrong way. I can't fight sin, or will my way to victory; I have to choose to let my flesh die.

Journal your thoughts:

_____
_____
_____
_____
_____
_____

BREAKOUT SESSION

Spiritual Weapons Against Lust

Despising and Mourning Our Sin

James 4:8-9 - Cleanse your hands, you sinners; and purify your hearts, you double-minded. Lament and mourn and weep! Let your laughter be turned to mourning and your joy to gloom.

CHAPTER 3 - YOU WON'T GET NO SATISFACTION

TWO THINGS THAT CANNOT BE SATISFIED

Proverbs 27:20 - Hell and destruction are never full; so the eyes of man are never satisfied.

We see two things in this verse that can never be satisfied, and they certainly are related to each other. They are death and sin. Hell and the grave are never satisfied, but are always craving more. Hell is a place of everlasting damnation and destruction that has received multitudes of souls already. There is still room for more in this place of torments, and it will not be full until the last day.

The lust for sin is never satisfied. The eyes of man are never satisfied, nor the appetites of the carnal mind towards profit and pleasure. Men seek that which does not satisfy. This has been true of every generation since our first parents were not satisfied with all the trees of Eden, and partook of the forbidden fruit.

It is only when we look to the Lord Jesus Christ, by faith, that we find satisfaction and peace of mind.

Now let's consider several truths relating to our text.

I. DEATH CANNOT BE SATISFIED - 'Hell and destruction are never full' (v. 20).

A. Countless millions have died since Adam's sin in The Garden.

1. Yet death is not satisfied, but still craves more victims to addiction.
2. Death is like the spiritual leach, a bloodsucking creature that never gets enough. Proverbs 30:15-16.

B. 'The wages of sin' have caused generations to be destroyed.
    1. The pit is still not full.
        a. Hell has opened his belly to swallow up the ungodly. Isaiah 5:14.
        b. The grave is like a wide and vast gulf, which at the command of God devours those who are condemned to die.
        c. Those that rebel against the Lord will be carried away by death.
            - Those that harden themselves against the Lord's chastisements will lose everything in which they have trusted.
    2. Hell still has room for those who are cast into it.
        a. Everlasting destruction is reserved for those that continue in their rebellion against the Lord. Isaiah 30:33.
        b. 'Tophet' speaks of God's highest curse, and it means Hell.
        c. It is the place where the wicked are shut up, as in a prison, after their death, in order to endure the excruciating torments that they deserve.
    3. In hell, the wrath of God will be like a continual stream of brimstone, keeping up the fire of it, so that it shall ever burn, and never be quenched.

a. This place of everlasting torments has been prepared for the devil and all that live in disobedience to the Lord. Matthew 25:41.

b. Hell it is called a lake burning with fire and brimstone; into which Satan, the beast, and false prophet, and the worshippers of antichrist, will be cast. Revelation 14:10; 19:20; 20:10; 21:8.

II. THE LUST FOR SIN CANNOT BE SATISFIED - So the eyes of man are never satisfied? (v. 20).

A. The lustful desires of man cannot be satisfied. The eyes (desires) of man are never satisfied.'

B. The desires of man are always requiring new gratification.
He enlargeth his desire as hell, and is as death, and cannot be satisfied? Habakkuk 2:5.

1. The sinner is never satisfied, but is always seeking to fulfill his lustful desires.

2. Because God is the judge of the entire world, He will sooner or later execute judgment upon the wicked.

C. Man seeks satisfaction in something short of God, because of his depraved heart.

1. He is always seeking for that ultimate SATISFACTION in earthly things.

a. This he will never find! Ecclesiastes 1:8.

b. The eternal soul can never be satisfied with temporal things.

2. All the affections of fallen man are filled with unquenched thirst.

a. Solomon had enjoyed all of the sensual pleasures of the world. Ecclesiastes 2:10.

b. Yet these worldly pleasures left him disappointed and dissatisfied. v. 11; 6:7.

c. The soul of man was originally created to find infinite satisfaction in the love of the Creator.

d. However, as a result of the Fall, man seeks to find satisfaction in things rather than the Creator.

III. ONLY THE LORD CAN SATISFY

A. The Lord has made us for Himself and there is no rest outside of KNOWING Him.

1. This is why the Lord Jesus invites sinners to find rest in Him.

2. The only source of true rest is to submit to the Lord Jesus Christ. Matthew 11:28-30.

B. The Fountain of Infinite Fullness is at the door of our heart. Psalm 4:6-8
- Only the Lord can satisfy our desires. Revelation 3:20.

1. He is the ever-living Water that satisfies. Isaiah 55:1-2, 6-7; Jn. 7:37; 6:35.

2. We find complete satisfaction only in our Lord. Lamentations 3:22-26.

3. To delight in anything other than the Lord is to remove Him from His throne and to dwell in misery.

CONCLUSION

- Only the Lord satisfies. Psalm 73:25-28.
- True satisfaction is found only in Christ.

- If we seek the Lord by faith today, we shall be eternally satisfied. Psalm 17:15.
- Those who have their eyes on the Lord shall be satisfied!

BREAKOUT SESSION

Spiritual Weapons Against Lust

Confessing My Sin and Seeking Forgiveness

1 John 1:9 - If we confess our sins, He is faithful and just to forgive us our sins and to cleanse us from all unrighteousness.

Psalm 32:5-6 - I acknowledged my sin to You, and my iniquity I have not hidden. I said, "I will confess my transgressions to the LORD," and You forgave the iniquity of my sin. For this cause everyone who is godly shall pray to You in a time when You may be found.

Jeremiah 8:22 - I sought God's forgiveness constantly, almost continuously, when I started to seriously battle lust. I rested in knowing that this did not displease God. The prophet Jeremiah questioned why his countrymen did not access the physician and "balm in Gilead" to receive healing and recovery.

Do we need to be asked this as well? Is there really any other solution?

It is precisely when we are intensely struggling to break loose from habitual sin that we need to quickly turn to God. He desires to forgive and "cleanse us from all unrighteousness."

_____

_____

_____

_____

_____

CHAPTER 4 - THE EYE GATES

Looking on a woman lustfully is adulterous. Matthew 5:27-28

Spiritual surgery may be needed to avoid immorality. Matthew 29-30

The primary gate to the entrance of lust to our heart is the eyes.

1.What the eye allows determines the nature of the traffic in the heart.

2.If your eye allows good traffic, your whole body is filled with light (Matthew 6:22).

3.If your eye is bad, your heart and body become full of darkness (Matthew 6:23).

4.When the eye gate is shut, the enemy is now on the outside of your heart and you can fight him from a place of advantage.

In the quest for purity, the real battleground is the battle for the heart. "Bringing every thought into captivity to the obedience of Christ" (2 Corinthians 10:5). An eye covenant equips us to fight that battle.

Stay on the Path

Proverbs 4:20-27

1. Vision is formed by teaching

2. Vision flows from the heart

3. Vision must be focused

Is your heart healthy?

_____
_____
_____
_____
_____
_____
_____
_____
_____

Verse 20 - "My son, attend to my words; Incline thine ear unto my sayings. Let them not depart from thine eyes; Keep them in the midst of thy heart. For they are life unto those that find them, And health to all their flesh. Keep thy heart with all diligence; For out of it are the issues of life. Put away from thee a wayward mouth, And perverse lips put far from thee. Let thine eyes look right on, And let thine eyelids look straight before thee. Make level the path of thy feet, And let all thy ways be established.

Turn not to the right hand nor to the left:

Remove thy foot from evil."

"My son, attend to my words" (Proverbs 4:20). It is just as reasonable to construe these words as being spoken by the teacher (or the father) during a given speech as it is to make them invariably the beginning of another discourse. Such an address could have come in the middle of an exhortation as the attention of the listener diminished and needed to be stimulated.

"Let them not depart from thine eyes" (Proverbs 4:21). This is exactly the same as Proverbs 3:21, another example of the constant repetition in Proverbs. "The repeated message is that, `it is not enough to hear wise instruction; it must be assimilated, pondered and kept at the center of man's being.'

"Keep thy heart with all diligence ... etc." (Proverbs 4:23). Here is another favorite verse which many have committed to memory. The heart, as the word is used in the Bible, means the mind, which is the center of human intelligence, emotions and the will. "The fact here stated is that the whole moral conduct of human life, and its every action, attitude and purpose are determined by what one thinks and believes." The great corollary of this is that "thought control" is the prerequisite of all moral rectitude and uprightness. See Proverbs 23:7.

"The last verses of this discourse are put together around the discipline of (1) the heart, (2) the mouth, (3) the eyes, and (3) the feet." This is true, but if one takes charge of his mind and controls his thoughts he is not likely to have much trouble with the other organs mentioned. The attainment of such power is greatly aided by the admonition of the apostle Paul (Philippians 4:8). "Whatsoever things are true ... honorable ... just ... pure ... lovely ... of good report ... any virtue ... any praise, THINK ON THESE THINGS"!

"Let thine eyelids look straight before thee ...turn not to the right hand nor to the left" (Proverbs 4:25,27). These instructions have found their way into the vernacular as, "Keep your eye on the ball, and stay in the middle of the road."! The great goal of earthly existence, for every wise man, is that of receiving at last the blessed welcome of the Lord, "Well done, thou good and faithful servant." Looking straight ahead means that men should not allow sensual, earthly, selfish, or material temptations to turn their eyes and their purpose away from the true goal and toward such other considerations. The mention of the right and the left hand is a warning against extreme positions. It should always be remembered that there is a ditch on either side, (the right or the left) of the road!

Distracted drivers not only have the potential to destroy their own lives, but the lives of others as well.

Watching in Prayer

The Lord has just warned his disciples that they will abandon him, and when Peter says that no matter what the others do, "he" will never abandon him. Jesus replies that before the cock crows you will three times. Peter says no that will never be the case and the Bible says, "so said they all" (Matthew 26:35).

The Lord and his disciples make their way to a place called Gethsemane (meaning oil press) it was the name of a garden on the eastern bank of the brook Kidron, it was probably located at the foot of the Mount of Olives about 3/4 of a mile form eastern wall of Jerusalem. According to Luke 22:39 it was Jesus' custom to go there to pray.

The Lord strengthens us in times of temptation as we believe His promises and seek His help (1 Corinthians 10:13).

• God is faithful to forgive our sins and cleanse us from all unrighteousness as we confess our sins to Him in prayer (1 John 1:9).

•Prayer is our source of guidance as we seek the Lord's direction and listen for His instructions (Ps. 32:8).

- God helps us understand His Word as we read and ask Him to speak to our hearts.

- Prayer is a shield that protects us from anxiety and worries when we remember that He has full control and provides the grace we need in every situation.

- Through prayer, the Lord gives us courage and confidence to face challenges, and reminds us that He puts sovereign limitations on the burdens we carry.

- Prayer brings God's emotional and physical healing as well as guidance when we're confused about the hurts we experience.

- We receive the Holy Spirit's power, which strengthens us to face difficult situations.

- Prayer can impact other people anywhere in the world because it creates a holy triangle between us, God, and whomever we pray for.

Keep Your Eyes on Jesus

Matthew 14:29,30 - And he said, Come. And when Peter was come down out of the ship, he walked on the water, to go to Jesus. But when he saw the wind boisterous, he was afraid; and beginning to sink, he cried, saying, Lord, save me.

What lesson did Peter learn about stepping out in faith? What can we learn from this about stepping out in faith?

_____

_____

_____

_____

_____

_____

_____

_____ '_____

_____

_____

- You got to keep your eyes on Jesus. If you look at the problems (the wind) you will become afraid, start to doubt and then sink.

- Peter had enough faith to get him out of the boat, but not enough to carry him across the water. At least Peter was wise enough to ask the Lord to save him.

- Our doubt is sometimes the limiting factor for faith to work. God's sovereignty is another factor.

- Jesus never rejects weak faith, but accepts it and builds on it.

- Faith is strengthened by being taken to extremities of what we have not faced before.

- What was the response of the disciples in the boat to the miracle they saw?

_____

_____

_____

_____

_____

_____

_____

_____

_____

_____

- They worshipped Jesus acknowledging that truly Jesus is the Son of God. The crowds were amazed when they saw a miracle but the disciples had by now gone past amazement to worship.

- God had announced at Jesus' baptism that Jesus was His own Son, the demons at Gadara addressed Him as the Son of God.

- But this is the first time that the disciples declare that Jesus is God's Son.

- Do you worship God when you see a miracle or are you just in awe? What kind of miracles do we fail to worship God for?

_____
_____
_____
_____
_____
_____
_____
_____
_____
_____

- I know I thank and praise God. I need to be more intentional on worshipping Him as well.

- There are many little miracles that happen in our life and maybe we take them for granted.

Even though the disciples obeyed Jesus and got into the boat, they faced a storm. Can we face storms too in life even if we are obedient to the Lord? How did God honor the disciple's obedience? Does God honor our obedience too?

_____

_____

_____

_____

_____

_____

_____

_____

_____

Addictions come in all shapes and sizes. Our "drug of choice" might be anything: spending, alcohol, drugs, pornography, affairs, food, people, jobs, even Christian service. They touch that part of our heart created for deep communion with God, offering enjoyment, relief from pain, or fulfillment, but they come with chains of bondage. These counterfeit lovers grab our hearts, demanding more and more, but never quenching our deepest thirsts.

Jesus longs for us to be free. He knows all about our past, our hurts, our destructive habits, and our addictions. He wants to set you free from all that. Jesus alone can heal our pain and fill our hearts with the one thing we were born searching for. Jesus' mission, explained in Isaiah 61:1-3, shows how much Jesus longs for each of us to be free:

He sent me to bind up the brokenhearted, to proclaim freedom for the captives and release from darkness for the prisoners, to proclaim the year of the LORD's favor and the day of vengeance of our God, to comfort all who mourn, to provide for those who grieve in Zion – to bestow on them the crown of beauty instead of ashes, the oil of gladness instead of mourning, and a garment of praise instead of a spirit of despair.

BREAKOUT SESSION

Spiritual Weapons Against Lust

Repenting From Our Sin

Romans 2:4 - Do you despise the riches of His goodness, forbearance, and longsuffering, not knowing that the goodness of God leads you to repentance?

Proverbs 28:13 - He who covers his sins will not prosper, but whoever confesses and forsakes them will have mercy.

Challenge: Habitual sin may overwhelm for a season and keep a perpetual hold on you as it wounds and infects you, but the treatment is the same whenever you stumble. We need to repent. Repenting includes giving up our past ways and thoughts. Are you prepared to do that?

_____

_____

_____

_____

_____

_____

_____

_____

_____

_____

_____

_____

_____

_____

_____

_____

_____

_____

CHAPTER 5 - TRAINING THE EYES

Job 31:1 - I made a covenant with mine eyes; why then should I think upon a maid?

Our Eyes are a Window into our Soul

There exists an old saying in American culture: "The eyes are a window to the soul." Jesus spoke about this when He taught on how our eyes reflect either spiritual light or great spiritual darkness within our souls.

Matthew 6:22-23 - The light of the body is the eye: if therefore thine eye be single, thy whole body shall be full of light. But if thine eye be evil, thy whole body shall be full of darkness. If therefore the light that is in thee be darkness, how great is that darkness.

Jesus makes certain that there is no misunderstanding; that either we are full of light or we are in great darkness. Just as we cannot love two masters, so that there cannot be any neutrality in the state of our souls.

How and what makes the difference between an eye full of light and an eye full of darkness? To know this you have to understand light and know where darkness comes from.

Spiritual Darkness:

Spiritual darkness came upon all mankind without exception in the Garden of Eden when Adam and Eve rebelled against God. Adam and Eve's pride drove them to eat of the tree of the knowledge of good and evil.

Romans 1:21 - Because that, when they knew God, they glorified him not as God, neither where thankful; but became vain in their imaginations, and their foolish heart was darkened.

Through Adam and Eve's sin and pride, mankind was thrust into "great" spiritual darkness and sadly, this darkness exists today.

From where comes the light?

_____

_____

_____

_____

_____

_____

_____

_____

_____

Jesus said in John 9 verse 5, "As long as I am in the world, I am the light of the world. "When Jesus went back to heaven He promised He would send another light: God, the Holy Spirit, also known as the Comforter.

John 15:26 - But when the Comforter is come, whom I will send unto you from the Father, even the Spirit of truth, which proceedeth from the Father, he shall testify of me.

The Holy Spirit comes to dwell within each person to whom the Father sends Him. His presence within us is the proof we have become one of God's people. If we are one of the blessed recipients of God's gift of salvation, the Spirit will remain in us forever.

John 14:16 - And I will pray the Father, and he shall give you another Comforter, that he may abide with you forever.

The Spirit is the light that rekindles the light that was darkened by our sin and the sin of Adam. Through the Spirit's presence and power each and every person in whom the Spirit dwells become the light of the world:

Matthew 5:14 - "Ye are the light of the world. A city that is set on a hill..." that cannot be hid.

This is now our purpose and task, if the Spirit of God dwells within us:

Matthew 5: 16 - Let your light so shine before men, that they may see your good works, and glorify your Father which is in heaven.

How are you bringing glory to the kingdom of God?

_____

_____

_____

_____

_____

_____

_____

_____

_____

_____

_____

_____

_____

_____

_____

_____

BREAKOUT SESSION

Spiritual Weapons Against Lust

Not Provisioning For Sin

Romans 13:14 - Put on the Lord Jesus Christ, and make no provision for the flesh, to fulfill its lusts.

1 Timothy 1:15 - Paul understood and explained sin like no other writer, no doubt since he himself had been an exceptional sinner – "I am the worst".

By singling out the concept of "provision," – providing for in advance – he directly highlighted the intricate mischief that the sin of lust thrives on.

While a slave to lust, I would pitiful dealing with the spiritual kryptonites of addiction in my life only to anticipate opportunities to feed it. This required a certain level of planning and anticipation. Paul speaks directly against this planning process to make no provision for the flesh.

_____

_____

_____

_____

_____

_____

_____

_____

_____

_____

_____

_____

_____

CHAPTER 6 - KEEP YOUR HEART

How do we become effective in the kingdom of God?

_____

_____

_____

_____

_____

_____

_____

_____

_____

_____

We must not only learn how the Kingdom operates, we must also learn how to reap from it. We can receive all that God has for us by doing things His way. He wants us to value His Word and plant it in our hearts just as a farmer plants seeds in the ground. We must guard and protect the Word until it produces results in our lives.

- "My son, attend to my words; consent and submit to my sayings" (Proverbs 4:20, AMP).

    1. When we give attention to God's Word, we are putting it in our hearts by hearing it, speaking it, and keeping it before our eyes (Proverbs 4:21, AMP).

        - We have dominion in this earth; therefore, we can receive word-seeds (either positive or negative) and grow them in our hearts.

- Giving attention to God's Word is the first step to "planting" it in our hearts as a seed.

2. "For they are life to those who find them, healing and health to all their flesh (Proverbs 4:22, AMP).

   - The Word, which is spiritual, can turn into a physical manifestation such as healing.

3. "Keep and guard your heart with all vigilance and above all that you guard, for out of it flow the springs of life" (Proverbs 4:23, AMP).

   - Whatever you look at, listen to, and speak about in abundance will eventually overwhelm and overtake your life.

   - Be sure the Word stays in your heart in abundance.

   - Do not speak words that oppose the Word of God (Proverbs 4:24, AMP).

   - Stay focused on the Word (Proverbs 4:25, AMP).

- "Thy word have I hid in mine heart, that I might not sin against thee" (Psalm 119:11).

1. We must do our part in making sure our heart is good ground, where the seed (God's Word) can be planted.

   - The Word of God should be hidden and protected in our hearts, just as a seed is hidden and protected in good soil.

Study Verses for Overcoming Lustful Desires:

Proverbs 4:23 - Keep thy heart with all diligence; for out of it are the issues of life.

Proverbs 4:24-27 - Put away from thee a froward mouth, and perverse lips put far from thee.

25 Let thine eyes look right on, and let thine eyelids look straight before thee.

26 Ponder the path of thy feet, and let all thy ways be established.

27 Turn not to the right hand nor to the left: remove thy foot from evil.

Matt. 15:19-20 - Put away from thee a froward mouth, and perverse lips put far from thee.

25 Let thine eyes look right on, and let thine eyelids look straight before thee.

26 Ponder the path of thy feet, and let all thy ways be established.

27 Turn not to the right hand nor to the left: remove thy foot from evil.

If we would be people "after God's own heart", then let us be careful to maintain the attitudes of repentance, worship, and service. This is what the Lord is looking for in all of us.

Acts 13:22 - After removing Saul, he made David their king. He testified concerning him: 'I have found David son of Jesse a man after my own heart; he will do everything I want him to do.'

The following words describe the heart of David as seen in his own writings:

Humble – Lowborn men are but a breath, the highborn are but a lie; if weighed on a balance, they are nothing; together they are only a breath. Psalm 62:9

Reverent – I call to the Lord, who is worthy of praise, and I am saved from my enemies. Psalm 18:3

Respectful – Be merciful to me, O Lord, for I am in distress; my eyes grow weak with sorrow, my soul and my body with grief. Psalm 31:9

Trusting – The LORD is my light and my salvation—whom shall I fear? The LORD is the stronghold of my life—of whom shall I be afraid? Psalm 27:1

Loving – I love you, O Lord, my strength. Psalm 18:1

Devoted – You have filled my heart with greater joy than when their grain and new wine abound. Psalm 4:7

Recognition – I will praise you, O Lord, with all my heart; I will tell of all your wonders. Psalm 9:1

Faithful – Surely goodness and love will follow me all the days of my life, and I will dwell in the house of the LORD forever. Psalm 23:6

Obedient – Give me understanding, and I will keep your law and obey it with all my heart. Psalm 119:34

Repentant – For the sake of your name, O Lord, forgive my iniquity, though it is great. Psalm 25:11

David's example is a great road map for how we are to live our life.

BREAKOUT SESSION

Spiritual Weapons Against Lust

Fleeing Temptation and Resisting the Very First Impulse to Sin

1 Corinthians 6:18 - Flee sexual immorality. Every sin that a man does is outside the body, but he who commits sexual immorality sins against his own body. Resist the devil and he will flee from you.

Even though I left the road well-traveled, I am still very much subject to ambush by temptation. This is inevitable and expected. However, such ambushes do not carry the same danger, power or draw that they once did. My defense is to instantly recoil from them. Such a response is possible because my heart and mind have not been mulched with layer upon layer of sin. New lusting does not take root.

I do not claim that I have developed any special ability or strength to endure temptation. Lust is such a powerful and swift sin that it can take hold very quickly. There is nothing to be gained by testing my strength or ability to resist. In any case, the battle is always entered into and decided at the very first impulse to sin. Will I give in or turn away? The story of Joseph fleeing the temptation of Potiphar's wife is a good example of this (Genesis 39).

Given an opportunity to turn our backs, we must make this our first defense. A foolhardy testing of our strength creates an uneven playing field that we are ill-equipped to enter. Fleeing physically, whenever possible, and certainly within the meditations of our hearts is the only effective strategy. This may wrongly be considered a sign of weakness. Instead it is simple obedience. How better can we obey the charge our Savior gave us?

We "flee" by refusing to linger physically, visually or mentally on that which could work itself into sin. Understanding the mechanics of lust and that it is not inevitable or forced upon us by the way God designed us keeps us aware that sin cannot play out unless we allow it. If we obey in this regard—actually doing that which we have been told to do—it acts as a practical evidence of our relationship with Christ.

1 John 2:3 - "By this we know that we know Him, if we keep His commandments".

1 Corinthians 10:13 - "No temptation has overtaken you except such as is common to man; but God is faithful, who will not allow you to be tempted beyond what you are able, but with the temptation will also make the way of escape, that you may be able to bear it".

Paul's statement seems foolish to those who consistently give in to the illicit sexual talk of the town, but to those who understand the gateway sin of adultery in the heart and begin to act in the way God desires, it proves true and reliable.

Ephesians 6:16 - It is by the "shield of faith" that we are "able to quench all the fiery darts of the wicked one".

Our faith is not self-generated or self-directed but rather, comes from God and is placed in Him. As we learn to fully trust in our Savior, and the instructions he laid out for us we will automatically avoid negative backward momentum from the sin (Kryptonites) He warned us against. Jesus knew that learning to do this may be difficult and therefor provides abundant help.

John 14:15-17 - "If you love Me, keep My commandments and I will pray the Father, and He will

give you another Helper, that He may abide with you
forever — the Spirit of truth".

_____
_____
_____
_____
_____
_____
_____
_____
_____
_____
_____
_____
_____
_____
_____
_____
_____
_____
_____
_____
_____
_____
_____
_____
_____
_____
_____
_____
_____
_____
_____
_____
_____
_____
_____
_____
_____

CHAPTER 7 - STAY STRONG - DISCERN YOUR DELILAH'S

Judges 14:1-3 - Then Samson went down to Timnah and saw a woman in Timnah, one of the daughters of the Philistines. 2 So he came back and told his father and mother, "I saw a woman in Timnah, one of the daughters of the Philistines; now therefore, get her for me as a wife." 3 Then his father and his mother said to him, "Is there no woman among the daughters of your relatives, or among all our people, that you go to take a wife from the uncircumcised Philistines?" But Samson said to his father, "Get her for me, for she looks good to me."

Judges 16:1 - Now Samson went to Gaza and saw a harlot there, and went in to her.

UNGODLY SOUL TIES – SCHOOL OF DELIVERANCE

What is a Soul Tie?

What is a soul tie?

_____

_____

_____

_____

_____

_____

_____

_____

_____

The Bible speaks of what is today known as soul ties. In the Bible, it doesn't use the word soul tie, but it speaks of them when it talks about souls being knit together, becoming one flesh, etc.

A soul tie can serve many functions, but in its simplest form, it ties two souls together in the spiritual realm. Soul ties between married couples draw them together like magnets, while soul ties between fornicators can draw a beaten and abused woman to the man which in the natural realm she would hate and run from, but instead she runs to him even though he doesn't love her, and he treats her like dirt.

In the demonic world, unholy soul ties can serve as bridges between two people to pass demonic garbage through. I helped a young man not too long ago break free from downright awful visitations from demons, all due to an ungodly soul tie he had with a witch. The man was a Christian, and the only thing that allowed her to send demonic torment his way, is through the soul tie. Other soul ties can do things such as allow one person to manipulate and control another person, and the other person is unaware to what is going on or knows what is going on, but for no real reason, allows it to continue.

How Soul Ties are Formed:

How do you believe soul ties are formed?

_____

_____

_____

_____

_____

_____

_____

_____

_____

I believe there are other ways which soul ties are formed, but here are some that I am aware of:

Sexual relations: Godly soul ties are formed when a couple are married.

Ephesians 5:31 - For this cause shall a man leave his father and mother, and shall be joined unto his wife, and they two shall be one flesh.

The Godly soul tie between a husband and wife that God intended them to have is unbreakable by man. (Mark 10:7-9).

However, when a person has ungodly sexual relations with another person, an ungodly soul tie is then formed.

1 Corinthians 6:16 - What? know ye not that he which is joined to an harlot is one body? for two, saith he, shall be one flesh.

This soul tie fragments the soul and is destructive. People who have many past relationships find it very difficult to 'bond' or be joined to anybody, because their soul is fragmented.

Close relationships: King David and Jonathan had a good soul tie as a result of a good friendship

1 Samuel 18:1 - And it came to pass, when he had made an end of speaking unto Saul, that the soul of Jonathan was knit with the soul of David, and Jonathan loved him as his own soul.

However, bad soul ties can form from bad relationships as well. Idolizing somebody can cause a bad soul tie. I have heard too that you can create a soul tie with gangs by becoming and close connection elicit actions ungodly behavior. This explains the strong pull towards certain music that seems almost irresistible.

Vows, commitments and agreements: Vows are known to bind the soul (Numbers 30:2), marriage itself consists of vows and binds the two people together (Ephesians 5:31), therefore I have little reason to overlook the concept of vows or commitments as being a means to create a soul tie.

How to Break a Soul Tie:

1. If any sins were committed to cause this soul tie, repent of them! Fornication is perhaps one of the most common ways to create nasty soul ties.
2. If gifts were given to you by the other person in connection with the sin or unholy relationship, such as rings, flowers, cards, bras, I would get rid of them! Such things symbolize the ungodly relationship, and can hold a soul tie in place. If you are still friends or in a relationship (just now it's no longer an ungodly relationship), like say a boyfriend/girlfriend relationship, except you've repented of and forsaken the unholy practices you used to do in your relationship, then I don't feel it is necessary to destroy all the gifts and things that you have been given. I would still encourage you to get rid of anything that symbolizes the ungodly practices in the relationship though, such as if a guy gives a girl a bra and panties with his initials on them during fornication. I wouldn't encourage you to hang on to such things that symbolize sin or that are wrong to give each other before marriage. Things such as flowers and love

letters given during an adultery should be destroyed.

3. Any rash vows or commitments made that played a part in forming the soul tie should be renounced and repented of, and broken in Jesus' name. Even things like "I will love you forever", or "I could never love another man!" need to be renounced. They are spoken commitments that need to be undone verbally. As Proverbs 21:23 tells us, "Whoso keepeth his mouth and his tongue keepeth his soul from troubles." The tongue has the ability to bring the soul great troubles and bondage.

4. Forgive that person if you have anything against them.

5. Renounce the soul tie. Do this verbally, and in Jesus' name. Example, "In Jesus' name, I now renounce any ungodly soul ties formed between myself and _____ as a result of _____ (fornication, etc.)."

6. Break the soul tie in Jesus' name! Do this verbally using your authority in Jesus. Example, "I now break and sever any ungodly soul ties formed between myself and _____ as a result of _____ (fornication, etc.) in Jesus' name."

Deliverance Prayers

For Breaking Soul Ties

Heavenly Father, I confess and repent of the sin of _____ (name the sin which caused the evil soul tie, such as adultery or fornication), and I ask that you forgive me of this sin.
[Now is a good time to destroy or get rid of any physical gifts or other objects that could hold the

soul tie together, such as a gift given in an adultery, etc. Anything that could hold the bond together between you and that person.]

In the name of Jesus, and by the power of His blood, I now renounce, break and sever all unholy soul ties formed between _____ (name the person) and myself, through the sin of _____ (name the sin which caused the evil soul tie, such as adultery or fornication).

I now command any evil spirits which have taken advantage of this unholy soul tie to leave me now in the name of Jesus!

(Repeat this prayer if you have more than one evil soul tie to break)

Renouncing Ungodly Vows

Heavenly Father, I repent and renounce the vow I made to _____ (name the demon or person, or even God, that you made the vow to) to preform _____ (describe what the vow entailed). I realize this was foolish and rash on my behalf, and I ask that you will forgive me and release me from the bondage that this vow has brought me under.

In the name of Jesus, and by the power of His blood, I now renounce, break and nullify the vow to _____ to perform _____, and I confess that I am released from this vow and it's bondage in Jesus' name.

I now command any evil spirits which have taken advantage of this unholy vow to leave me now in the name of Jesus!

(Repeat this prayer if you have more than one unholy vow to break).

Renounce Involvement with Unhealthy (demonic) Music

Heavenly Father, I confess that I used to listen to unhealthy demonic music. I ask that you will forgive and cleanse me from this sin.

In the name of Jesus, and through the power of His blood, I now renounce, break and sever all soul ties that have been formed between myself and the unhealthy music (name specific songs and artists/groups if possible) I used to listen to and enjoy, as well as any soul ties formed between myself and the artists and groups (name them specifically if possible) and demonic influences that have produced these unhealthy songs and music.

In Jesus' name, I also renounce, break and nullify any curses that I may have come under as a result of listening to the unhealthy music I used to listen to and enjoy.

In the name of Jesus, I now command all evil spirits to leave me that have taken advantage of these soul ties I have just renounced. In the name of Jesus, I also renounce and command any evil spirits that have taken advantage of any curses that I have come under as a result of listening to unhealthy music to leave me now in Jesus' name! I also renounce and command any evil spirits that have entered me through my listening to this unhealthy music to leave me now in the name of Jesus'!

Breaking Generational Curses

In the name of Jesus, I confess the sins and iniquities of my parents (name specific sins if known), grandparents (name specific sins if known), and all other ancestors.

In the name of Jesus, and by the power of His blood, I now renounce, break and sever all cords of iniquity and generational curses I have inherited from my parents, grandparents and all other ancestors and break and sever all unholy soul ties formed between myself and my parents, grandparents and all other ancestors.

In the name of Jesus, I now loose myself and my future generations from any bondages passed down to me from my ancestors and I command any evil spirits which have taken advantage of these cords of iniquity, generational curses and unholy soul ties to leave me now in the name of Jesus!

BREAKOUT SESSION

Spiritual Weapons Against Lust

Reconciling Relationships

Matthew 5:24 - First be reconciled to your brother, and then come and offer your gift.

Ephesians 5:28-29 - So husbands ought to love their own wives as their own bodies; he who loves his wife loves himself. For no one ever hated his own flesh, but nourishes and cherishes it, just as the Lord does the church.

_____

_____

_____

_____

_____

_____

_____

_____

_____

_____

_____

_____

_____

CHAPTER 8 - STAY PURE - SINGLES MINISTRY

Symptoms of those who tend to struggle with singleness in life include difficulties with:

- Identity ("Who am I?" "What is my purpose?"); (Ephesians 2:10)
- Loneliness ("I need someone to share my life." "I feel so alone."); (Hebrews 13:5)
- Rejection ("I am not wanted." "I must not be lovable."); (1 John 3:1)
- Fear ("I will be all alone when I am old." "I don't want to be hurt ever again."); (Isaiah 41:10)
- Bitterness ("I am not receiving the best in life." "God must be punishing me."); (Psalm 84:11)
- Sexuality ("A sexual relationship is the only means to intimacy." "I don't know what to do with my sexual desires."); (Romans 12:1)
- Self-Worth ("I don't feel valuable." "I am not worthy enough to be loved."); (Isaiah 43:4)
- In our Singleness to the Lord, we should all allow ourselves to focus on being content and the Lord's content in our relationship with Him.
- Focus on pleasing the Lord. (1 Corinthians 7:32)
- Have undivided devotion to the Lord. (1 Corinthians 7:34-35)
- Singleness can be the happier state. (1 Corinthians 7:40)

BREAKOUT SESSION

Spiritual Weapons Against Lust

Rejoicing in My Wife

Proverbs 5:15-21 - Drink water from your own cistern,
And running water from your own well.
Should your fountains be dispersed abroad,
Streams of water in the streets?
Let them be only your own,
And not for strangers with you.
Let your fountain be blessed,
And rejoice with the wife of your youth.
As a loving deer and a graceful doe,
Let her breasts satisfy you at all times;
And always be enraptured with her love.
For why should you, my son, be enraptured by an
immoral woman,
And be embraced in the arms of a seductress?
For the ways of man are before the eyes of the LORD,
And He ponders all his paths.

_____
_____
_____
_____
_____
_____
_____
_____
_____
_____
_____
_____
_____
_____
_____
_____
_____
_____
_____
_____
_____

CHAPTER 9 - SEX IS GOD-GIVEN

Due Benevolence is very important to both the man and the woman in a marriage.

1Corinthians 7:3-5 - "Let the husband render unto the wife due benevolence: and likewise also the wife unto the husband. The wife hath not power of her own body, but the husband: and likewise also the husband hath not power of his own body, but the wife. Defraud ye not one the other, except it be with consent for a time, that ye may give yourselves to fasting and prayer; and come together again, that Satan tempt you not for your incontinency".

1 Peter 3:7 - Likewise, ye husbands, dwell with them according to knowledge, giving honour unto the wife, as unto the weaker vessel, and as being heirs together of the grace of life; that your prayers be not hindered.

What is Due Benevolence?

Due Benevolence has two meanings: (1) a General meaning and (2) a Technical meaning.

1. The Greek Word for Due Benevolence is Eunoia, which is a combination of two words, eu and noia. Eu means = good; while noia means mind. So, Eunoia (Due Benevolence) means Good-Mind. It also means good thinking, or ability to think before you act.

2. Other translations for Due Benevolence:

- The BBE Translation calls is 'what is right'

- GNB Translation calls it 'duty'

- ASV calls it 'Dues'

- Other translations call it what is 'owed' and yet others used the term 'what is appropriate' or 'what is acceptable'.

3. Summarily, Due Benevolence means:

- Husband and wife having a good mind towards one another to paying their dues (vows and promises) or what they owe each other (1Corinthians 7:4).

- Ability for husband and wife to think before they act.

The Question is: What do you owe your spouse?

_____
_____
_____
_____
_____
_____
_____
_____
_____

Below are some of the things that husband and wife owe one another:

1. COMPANIONSHIP:

Genesis 2:24 - Therefore shall a man LEAVE his father and his mother, and shall CLEAVE unto his wife: and they shall be ONE flesh.

Leaving + Cleaving = One Flesh (Matthew 19:5-6). Companionship can only occur when leaving and cleaving are properly done. Some leave their parents, but don't cleave to their spouse. It is not only good to leave, it's important to cleave.

Leaving without cleaving cannot bring companionship.

When there is cleaving then Ephesians 5:28 will be in force.

2. COMMUNICATION:

Good communications make good manners. Communicate your commendations and frustrations lovingly. Salty food. Dirty rooms

> *1Corinthians15:33 - Be not deceived: evil communications corrupt good manners.*

Express your love. Say words that that will set the atmosphere and start the morning with communication and before the nighttime activation of intimacy.

3. COMMUNION/FELLOWSHIP:

Spend time together in other areas of your home such as the kitchen and sitting room. Those who pray together stay together. Discuss church message and bible verses

4. COMPASSION:

Be there for better, for worse. Be there in sickness and health, through thick and thin.

5. ROMANCE/AFFECTIONS

You don't have power over your body.

> *1Corinthians 7:4-5 - The wife hath not power of her own body, but the husband: and likewise also the husband hath not power of his own body, but the wife. [5] Defraud ye not one the other, except it be with consent for a time, that ye may give yourselves to fasting and prayer; and come together again, that Satan tempt you not for your incontinency.*

Women respond to touch, men to look. Women need to be prepared long time, no sudden action. Don't be in a hurry when together with a woman. Foreplay, main play, after play.

6. CONTENTMENT/ COMMITMENT:

Prov. 5:19 - Let her breast satisfy thee.

Appreciate her work with the children, the kitchen, and the house chores. Be content with who your spouse is and what you have. Do everything with passion. See each other's vision. You need short term and long term goals.

7. CARE / GENTLE:

In other words - Avoid rape. Remember that she is fragile, so handle with care.

1Peter 3:7 - Likewise, ye husbands, dwell with them according to knowledge, giving honour unto the wife, as unto the weaker vessel, and as being heirs together of the grace of life; that your prayers be not hindered.

Sex is important but we should not be in lust for our spouse, but in love with their spouse. There will be times when you just cuddle, talk, or just hold hands. The most important thing is to enjoy what God created and safeguard yourself from the spiritual kryptonites that try to entice you.

I always go the extra mile to please my spouse. I have found out that just cleaning the house, offering solid communication, and spending quality time together is a lot easier when the atmosphere is set. We set the atmosphere that God designed us to live in embraced with love.

Once in a committed relationship and marriage, there's no rush for the sex. It all comes when both parties fill the role that is due to each other.

There should be no sexless marriage unless there is a major medical issue. Couples need to render their spirit to God into their spouse. Lovemaking doesn't start in the bedroom. It starts with attitude, atmosphere, respect, and gentleness which leads to enjoyable intimacy in the bedroom. That keeps the matrimony bed undefiled and holy.

Some time back, there was a thread about sex in marriage.

Psalm 63 presented a case where Paul was saying that sex needed to be done with benevolence.

Here is the passage in the KJV, which uses 'due benevolence'.

1 Corinthians 7:2-5 - Nevertheless, to avoid fornication, let every man have his own wife, and let every woman have her own husband. Let the husband render unto the wife due benevolence: and likewise also the wife unto the husband.

The wife hath not power of her own body, but the husband: and likewise also the husband hath not power of his own body, but the wife.

Defraud ye not one the other, except it be with consent for a time, that ye may give yourselves to fasting and prayer; and come together again, that Satan tempt you not for your incontinency.

Psalm 63

This scripture has a lot to do with intimacy in holiness and seeking God. If we value our relationships like we value the Word of God, we will reap the best results of intimacy. Give yourself 100% to do the best you can do in your relationship. I love the Word of God which will help you protect your garden.

Psalm 63 - A Psalm of David, when he was in the wilderness of Judah. O God, thou art my God; early will I seek thee: my soul thirsteth for thee, my flesh longeth for thee in a dry and thirsty land, where no water is; To see thy power and thy glory, so as I have seen thee in the sanctuary.

Because thy loving-kindness is better than life, my lips shall praise thee. Thus will I bless thee while I live: I will lift up my hands in thy name. My soul shall be satisfied as with marrow and fatness; and my mouth shall praise thee with joyful lips: When I remember thee upon my bed, and meditate on thee in the night watches.

Because thou hast been my help, therefore in the shadow of thy wings will I rejoice. My soul followeth hard after thee: thy right hand upholdeth me. But those that seek my soul to destroy it, shall go into the lower parts of the earth. They shall fall by the sword: they shall be a portion for foxes. But the king shall rejoice in God; every one that sweareth by him shall glory: but the mouth of them that speak lies shall be stopped.

- Do benevolence, not a sexless marriage – Hebrews 3:4
- Fulfill your duties to your spouse - 1 Corinthian's 7:3
- Your body belongs to your spouse – 1 Corinthian's 7:4

- Refrain only by mutual consent; for refraining can lead to temptation.
- Find satisfaction in your spouse - Proverbs 5:18-20

Is Lust Ever Worth Breaking Up Your Marriage?

God's solution to problems in your marriage is for you to:

First, make a commitment to please the Lord in all things (Colossians 1:10).

1. Examine and judge your own failures in a biblical manner, do not blame shift (1 Corinthians 11:28-31)

2. Confess your sin to the Lord and confess your marital shortcomings as sin to your spouse (1 John 1:9)

3. Seek to edify your spouse biblically and do it heartily as unto the Lord (Rom. 14:19 ; Rom. 15:1-2)

4. Seek to resolve conflicts and live at peace with your spouse. If your spouse refuses to resolve problems biblically, continue to trust in Christ Jesus for your peace and joy.

5. Work Out Your Salvation (Philippians 2:12-13)

Memory Verse(s):

Philippians 2:3-4 - Let nothing be done through strife or vainglory; but in lowliness of mind let each esteem other better than themselves.

4 Look not every man on his own things, but every man also on the things of others.

BREAKOUT SESSION

Spiritual Weapons Against Lust

Uprooting All Spiritual Pride

1 Corinthians 10:12 - Therefore let him who thinks he stands take heed lest he fall.

While overcome by habitual sin, the natural response is to feel guilt. As this guilt passes and we begin to gain victory, we must in turn guard against false confidence. There were times, especially early on, when this crept in and caused me to stumble in Sin & Shame failing short of the Glory. It is disappointing and surprising how I continue to be bothered by temptation at times and even stumble back.

_____

_____

_____

_____

_____

_____

_____

_____

_____

_____

_____

_____

_____

_____

_____

_____

_____

_____

_____

_____

CHAPTER 10 - A BED UNDEFILED

I like to dedicate this chapter to the married couples that say together in spite of the trials and tribulations of marriage.

This chapter can only cover a few basics concerning Christian marriage.

1. Marriage is worth the investment.

2. You have to invest in a marriage for it to be worth the investment.

3. Choosing your marriage partner is the most important human decision you will ever make.

4. Most fights are over stupid things that don't matter.

5. Most arguments are resolved when both people are more concerned with being in a relationship than with being right.

6. Sex is essential to a marriage relationship.

7. Practices (like date nights, long conversations, and trips together) make your marriage stronger.

8. Kids are awesome, but stress your marriage.

9. Never go to bed angry.

10. We need Jesus in his word it is the best way to resolve conflict.

Hebrews 13:4 - Marriage is honorable in all, and the bed undefiled: but whoremongers and adulterers God will judge.

Mark 10:6-9 But from the beginning of the creation God made them male and female. For this cause shall a man leave his father and mother, and cleave to his wife; and they twain shall be one flesh: so then they are no more twain, but one flesh. What therefore God hath joined together, let not man put asunder.

From the very beginning, God's will for marriage was and still is, between a man and a woman. God has sanctified this union and says that it is undefiled.

God's plan of sexual union between a man and a woman was not only for pro creation but also one of mutual love and satisfaction. Sex outside of the bond of marriage is called "fornication" or "adultery".

Sex between the same sex "homosexuality" is called an abomination to God. Abomination means something that is disgusting to God.

Leviticus 18:22 - Thou shalt not lie with mankind, as with womankind: it is abomination.

Romans 1:27 - The males in the same way also left natural sexual intercourse with females and were inflamed in their lust for one another. Males committed shameless acts with males and received in their own persons the appropriate penalty for their perversion.

1 Corinthians 6:9 - Do you not know that the unjust will not inherit God's kingdom? Do not be deceived: no sexually immoral people, idolaters, adulterers, male prostitutes, homosexuals

Duties of Husbands

1. Be satisfied with your wife

Proverbs 5:18-19 - Let thy fountain be blessed: and rejoice with the wife of thy youth. Let her be as the loving hind and pleasant roe; let her breast satisfy thee at all times; and be thou ravished always with her love.

Ecclesiastes 9:9 - Live joyfully with the wife whom thou lovest all the days of the life of thy vanity, which he hath given thee under the sun, all the days of thy vanity: for that is thy portion in this life, and in thy labor which thou takest under the sun.

2. Love his wife

Ephesians 5:28 - So ought men to love their wives as their own bodies. He that loveth his wife loveth himself.

Colossians 3:19 - Husbands, love your wives, and be not bitter against them. Give affection to his wife

1 Corinthians 7:3-5 - Let the husband render to his wife the affection that is due her, and likewise also the wife to her husband. The wife does not have authority over her own body, but the husband does. And likewise the husband does not have authority over his own body, but the wife does. Do not deprive one another except with consent for a time, that you may give yourselves to fasting and prayer.

3. Give honor to his wife

1 Peter 3:7 - Likewise ye husbands, dwell with them according to knowledge, giving honor unto the wife, as unto the weaker vessel, and as being heirs together of the grace of life; that your prayers be not hindered.

4. Provide for his wife

Genesis 3:19 - In the sweat of thy face shalt thou eat bread, till thou return unto the ground; for out of it wast thou taken: for dust thou art, and unto dust shalt thou return.

1 Timothy 5:8 - But if any provide not for his own, and specially for those of his own house, he m hapath denied the faith, and is worse than an infidel.

Headship of Husbands

Established by God

Genesis 3:16 - Unto the woman he said, I will greatly multiply thy sorrow and thy conception; in sorrow thou shalt bring forth children; and thy desire shall be to thy husband, and he shall rule over thee.

1 Corinthians 11:3 - But I would have you know, that the head of every man is Christ; and the head of the woman is the man; and the head of Christ is God.

Ephesians 5:23 - For the husband is head of the wife, even as Christ is head of the church: and he is savior of the body.

Duties of Wives

1. Give affection

1 Corinthians 7:3-5 - Let the husband render to his wife the affection due her, and likewise also the wife to her husband.

2. Submit to Husband

Ephesians 5:22 - Wives, submit yourselves unto your own husbands, as unto the Lord.

Colossians 3:18 - Wives, submit yourselves unto your own husbands, as it is fit in the Lord.

Submission does not mean inferior it only means to yield. We all submit in one way or another. In the USA we drive on the right side of the road, in a sense we are submitting to the laws of the land. It is when we refuse to submit, that we get into trouble.

I would ask you, is it wrong to drive on the established side of the road? Does it not prevent us from having head on collisions with other vehicles?

_____
_____
_____
_____
_____
_____
_____
_____
_____
_____

Do we not yield to established authorities such as Parents, Teachers, Police, Traffic signs, in doing so we keep harmony? There are guidelines and boundaries that are put in place for us to obey.

If a husband treats his wife with love and respect and assumes his position as the head of the home (with a servants heart) then he will not have to demand that his wife yields, she should be willing.

3. Not to usurp the husbands authority

1 Timothy - 2:11-12 Let a woman learn in silence with all submission. And I do not permit a woman to teach, nor to usurp authority over a man but to be in silence.

4. Be keepers at home

Titus 2:3-5 - The aged women likewise, that they be in behavior as becometh holiness, not false accusers, not given to much wine, teachers of good things; Vs.4 That they may teach the young women to be sober, to love their husbands, to love their children,
To be discreet, chaste, keepers at home, good, obedient to their own husbands, that the word of God be not blasphemed.

Journal your thoughts concerning this chapter.

_____
_____
_____
_____
_____
_____
_____
_____
_____
_____

What has made your marriage successful?

_____
_____
_____
_____
_____
_____
_____
_____
_____
_____

Marriage is honorable in all, and the bed undefiled: but whoremongers and adulterers God will judge.

Lust will defeat any man or any woman. It will destroy your marriage it will destroy your soul.

Sexual perversion includes a dollar tree, fornication, etc... a history of these sexual scenes in the bloodline open the door of curses of lust.

Christ has redeemed us from the curse of the law, being made a curse for us: for it is written 'cursed is everyone that hang it up on a tree'.

Colossians 3: 1-2; 5; 12-14 - "If then you have been raised with Christ, seek the things that are above, where Christ is, seated at the right hand of God.

2 Set your minds on things that are above, not on things that are on earth.

5 Put to death therefore what is earthly in you: sexual immorality, impurity, passion, evil desire, and covetousness, which is idolatry.

12 Put on then, as God's chosen ones, holy and beloved, compassionate hearts, kindness, humility, meekness, and patience, 13 bearing with one another and, if one has a complaint against another, forgiving each other; as the Lord has forgiven you, so you also must forgive. 14 And above all these put on love, which binds everything together in perfect harmony."

Often times we are drawn away from our own lust and if we don't repent and take notice it will lead to an affair which will defile the marriage bed.

Read and Journal your thoughts:

_____
_____
_____
_____
_____
_____
_____
_____
_____

John 8:1-11 - Jesus went to the mount of Olives: And early in the morning he came again into the temple, and all the people came to him; and he sat down and taught them. And the scribes and Pharisees brought to him a woman taken in adultery: and when they had set her in the midst, They say to him, Master, this woman was taken in adultery, in the very act. Now Moses in the law commanded us, that such should be stoned; but what sayest thou? This they said, tempting him, that they might have to accuse him. But Jesus stooped down, and with his finger wrote on the ground, as though he heard them not. So when they continued asking him, he raised himself, and said to them, He that is without sin among you, let him first cast a stone at her. And again he stooped down, and wrote on the ground. And they who heard it, being convicted by their own conscience, went out one by one, beginning at the eldest, even to the last: and Jesus was left alone, and the woman standing in the midst. When Jesus had raised himself, and saw none but the woman, he said to her, Woman, where are those thy accusers? hath no man condemned thee? She said, No man, Lord. And Jesus said to her, Neither do I condemn thee: go, and sin no more.

When they brought the woman to Jesus, the religious leaders were trying to trap Him. What was the penalty for anyone caught in adultery?

_____

_____

_____

_____

_____

_____

_____

_____

Who established this law?

_____
_____
_____
_____
_____
_____
_____

If Jesus let the woman go, of what would they accuse Him?

_____
_____
_____
_____
_____
_____
_____

If He punished her, of what would they accuse Him?

_____
_____
_____
_____
_____
_____

In what way were the religious leaders themselves "breaking the law"?

_____
_____
_____
_____

_____
_____
_____
_____

Do the religious leaders care about the woman?
Why or why not?

_____
_____
_____
_____
_____
_____
_____

How do you think the woman felt when they
made her stand before the crowd and publicly
announced her sin?

_____
_____
_____
_____
_____
_____
_____

How do you feel when someone publicly or
privately exposes a sin in your life?

_____
_____
_____
_____
_____
_____
_____

In verse 6 we are told Jesus knelt down and wrote on the ground. There is no way of knowing for sure, but what do you think Jesus was writing?

_____
_____
_____
_____
_____
_____
_____
_____

Imagine yourself in the crowd, feeling perfectly justified condemning the woman. How would you react to Jesus' remark in v. 7?

_____
_____
_____
_____
_____
_____
_____
_____

Can we apply this "principle" to our lives today? If so, what and how?

_____
_____
_____
_____
_____
_____
_____
_____

Why do you think the older ones were the first to leave?

_____
_____
_____
_____
_____
_____
_____
_____

What do you think the younger ones were thinking as the older ones began to leave?

_____
_____
_____
_____
_____
_____
_____

What do you thing they were thinking when they were the only ones left?

_____
_____
_____
_____
_____
_____
_____

As the crowd began to leave, what do think the woman was feeling?

_____
_____
_____
_____
_____

_____

_____

_____

Can you remember a time when you were
definitely wrong and someone forgave you? How
did that make you feel?

_____

_____

_____

_____

_____

_____

_____

_____

What did Jesus' forgiveness do for this guilty
woman?

_____

_____

_____

_____

_____

_____

_____

_____

What can we learn about confession of sin from
this episode?

_____

_____

_____

_____

_____

_____

_____

What can we learn about forgiveness?

_____

_____

_____

_____

_____

_____

_____

_____

Why are more eager to condemn other people's sins rather than our own?

_____

_____

_____

_____

_____

_____

_____

How would you describe Jesus' attitude toward women (vv 10-11)?

_____

_____

_____

_____

_____

_____

_____

To safeguard ourselves against adultery, we need to result to the word of God.

God will forgive the adulterous. Read

Scripture: "You shall not commit adultery." (Exodus 20:14)

The Four Phases of an Affair
  1. Accepting sinful thoughts in your mind.

_____

2. Emotional involvement
3. Physical involvement
4. You begin to rationalize the affair

Deuteronomy 22:22 - If a man is found sleeping with another man's wife, both the man who slept with her and the woman must die. You must purge the evil from Israel.

The PATHWAY Back To Purity

I. The PROBLEM of Adultery

"Marriage should be honored by all, and the marriage bed kept pure, for God will judge the adulterer"

A. You acknowledge your sin.
"O loving and kind God, have mercy...take away the awful stain of my transgressions... cleanse me from this guilt. Let me be pure again. For I admit my shameful deed--it haunts me day and night. It is against You that I have sinned...You saw it all..." (Psalm 51:1-4, LB)

B. You end the relationship immediately!
"I tell you, now is the time of God's favor, now is the day of salvation." (2 Corinthians 6:2) C. You do whatever it takes to avoid all contact with that person from now on!

"No test or temptation that comes your way is beyond the course of what others have had to face. All you need to remember is that God will never let you down; he'll never let you be pushed past your limit; he'll always be there to help you come through it."

(1 Corinthians 10:13, Msg)

God can give you the power to live pure and to keep your commitment to practicing sexual purity.

Adultery is a Trap

(Hebrews 13:4) (Proverbs 22:14)

Seven Causes of Adultery and Affairs

1. Unmet needs
2. Unfulfilled expectations
3. Underdeveloped self-esteem
4. Unresolved conflict
5. Uncontrolled thoughts
6. Unprotected life-style
7. UNRELIABLE COMMITMENT

Adultery begins in the head long before it gets in the bed.

You need a moral and spiritual commitment to Jesus Christ as the center of your marriage.

BREAKOUT SESSION

Spiritual Weapons Against Lust

Continuing in Prayer

Matthew 26:41 - Watch and pray, lest you enter into temptation. The spirit indeed is willing, but the flesh is weak.

Prayer stands out as the most direct outworking of being in Christ. It is by prayer that we confess our sins, seek forgiveness, worship God, and express our needs. When we abide in Christ and His words abide in us, our inner lives take on the form of an ongoing conversation with God. Prayer produces Forward momentum.

_____

_____

_____

_____

_____

_____

CHAPTER 11 - TRANSPARENCY

Those in early recovery are often still plagued with addictive thinking. That's why accountability is so important.

It is important that we make every attempt to safeguard our self from the pitfalls of our past. There is such Freedom when you live this way!!!

Galatians 5:1 - It was for freedom that Christ set us free; therefore keep standing firm and do not be subject again to a yoke of slavery.

- Don't be enslaved to lust

- Don't be enslaved to the secrets of your past

- Don't be enslaved to your guilt of past sin

- Don't be enslaved to your fear of repentance of past sin

This is living the abundant life in Jesus name!!!

This is the best life you can ever live under the power of God's word!!!

Practice of Transparency in Marriage

I am married to a Proverbs 31 woman. I trust her with all of my heart. We are approaching our 30th year of marriage. Life has its ups and downs, but we are still together by the grace of God. It is because of God's grace and His mercy which allowed us to stay together - it was love and forgiveness that kept us together.

I'm not saying that our marriage is perfect. I'm only suggesting that we should continue to stay in God's will and to work towards transparency.

Writing these books has been a blessing to me and allowed me to look into my life through the Word of God. I need to have a heart to continually change the closed doors of my past and safeguard myself for my destiny. It has been my desire to be transparent with you.

When we are living for Christ and we make every attempt to please Him, there will always be some battles, there will always be some fights, but when we keep God first in our life, we shall be more than conquerors. My wife and I have experienced the worst of times in our life dealing with my addictions. It was Jesus Christ that is brought us to the best of times. We are growing closer to God and to each other trusting in his Word and in each other.

T: Take time together

R: Reach out in love

U: Understand your spouse

S: Selflessly serve your spouse

T: Take the Risk

In the end, transparency will only happen if you are secure in who you are and, even more, you have to have your identity in Christ.

Picture of Christ

- God knows you completely.

- He knows everything there is to know about you.

- He knows you better than you know yourself.

- He knows every word you have ever spoken

- He knows every thought you have ever thought

- He knows every fantasy you have ever had

- He knows your motives

Hebrews 4:12-13 - For the word of God is living and active and sharper than any two-edged sword, and piercing as far as the division of soul and spirit, of both joints and marrow, and able to judge the thoughts and intentions of the heart.

And there is no creature hidden from His sight, but all things are open and laid bare to the eyes of Him with whom we have to do.

- The one who knows you best loves you most!!!

- God desires for you to get honest with Him!!!

- God wants you to have faith in Him!!!

- And when you were at your worst He loved you even then!!

Romans 5:6-8 - For while we were still helpless, at the right time Christ died for the ungodly. For one will hardly die for a righteous man; though perhaps for the good man someone would dare even to die. But God demonstrates His own love toward us, in that while we were yet sinners, Christ died for us.

- God wants a real relationship with you

- He knows you and your secrets

- God wants to reveal secrets to you

Psalm 25:12-14 - Who is the man who fears the LORD? He will instruct him in the way he should choose. His soul will abide in prosperity, And his descendants will inherit the land. The secret of the

LORD is for those who fear Him, And He will make them know His covenant.

He wants to tell you great and mighty things you do not know.

Like Adam in the Garden is God calling "where are you?"

_____
_____
_____
_____
_____
_____
_____
_____
_____

Is there shame that keeps you from coming to the Lord?

_____
_____
_____
_____
_____
_____
_____
_____
_____

How many have not opened up to Him?

_____
_____
_____

_____

_____

_____

_____

_____

_____

_____

_____

How many will not step out and come because
you are afraid of what people will think about
you?

_____

_____

_____

_____

_____

_____

_____

_____

_____

_____

_____

Transparency in Addiction Recovery

- It provides an outlet for you to be open and
  honest about your thoughts and feelings.
  Confiding in someone else means you do
  not have to keep everything bottled up
  inside.

- Your story may inspire someone else to get
  the help they need. Hearing about your
  experience can give them the strength to
  confront their addiction or help someone
  else to.

- Opening up can give you more confidence
  in your recovery and help you to see how far
  you have come.

- It can build stronger connections and help you not feel alone in your journey. Building a recovery community is important and takes time. Opening up to even just one person starts this process.

The ability to conceal your activities makes it easier and more likely for you to give in to the urges of addiction. If you can keep your behavior a secret, you can be fairly sure there will be no consequences – no anger, sadness, disapproval, or disappointment from your spouse; no loss of your family's trust and respect. Without those consequences, your struggle becomes a match of your willpower against your brain's chemical needs. When you can tell yourself "no one will ever know," you weaken your willpower's side of that fight. Think of accountability – and therefore think of transparency – as backup and support for your willpower in that fight.

Motivational accountability is choosing to be honest with another person or group of people about the desires and thoughts that truly drive and move us. This is about getting to the "sin beneath the sin." It may not even be sin of which we are consciously aware, so we need another set of eyes to help us see what we cannot. Motivational accountability requires really knowing one another and asking the hard heart questions. Are we fascinated with Christ and the gospel? Do I find great joy in God? What do we desire more than anything else? What do we find ourselves daydreaming or fantasizing about? Do we covet anything? Do we think more about how we can serve ourselves or how we can boast in Christ and serve others? Are we holding on to bitterness? Where do our thoughts drift to when we enter social settings? Where do our thoughts take us when we are all alone? What lies do we believe that continually drive us to disobey God? Do we love anything more than God?

Accountability Partners in Recovery

There are no limits when you have an accountability partner. Someone who holds you responsible for your actions and goals. Holds your hand through the sweat and tears. The results could bring out the best in both of you.

- remember and summarize the temptations you have faced, the choices you have made, and the state of your heart;

- discuss these matters with trusted Accountability Partners;

- talk concretely with others about ways to guard against sinful actions, thoughts, and motives; and

- see your need for the gospel—God's grace for overcoming both the guilt and the grip of sin.

ACCOUNTABILITY:

Having a person who knows enough about us to ask the right, sometimes hard, questions will help us be successful. Those in early recovery are often still plagued with addictive thinking. That's why accountability is so important.

PRIDE:

Ego, grandiosity, and self-centeredness ("I can do this all by myself, I don't need help from anyone")will get in the way of recovery. There is an ancient proverb that says, "Pride goes before a fall." Ultimately, an AP helps us to keep from getting trapped by our own false sense of "powerfulness" or "powerlessness" and keeps us humble.

HONESTY:

It's really easy to fool others and even ourselves. We've learned how to look really good on the outside while we're doing terrible on the inside. Here again, if we've been open with our AP about our personal issues, they will hold us accountable and confront us when we've slipped into dishonesty.

BREAKOUT SESSION

Spiritual Weapons Against Lust

Maintaining Transparency with Others Who Are Committed to Help

James 5:16 - Confess your sins to one another, and pray for one another, that you may be healed. The effective, fervent prayer of a righteous man avails much.

This was not a battle that I needed to fight alone. Many others are going through the same struggles and I needed their help.

My deliverance was brought about with the essential help of Christian brothers and spiritual fathers and only by the power of God. Becoming intentionally transparent about this subject, which is discussed so infrequently, resulted in many kinds of blessing. Such purposeful sharing can only succeed when we are focused on gaining victory and seeking a purity that aligns with what God expects. Being prayed for, praying for others, confessing failure, admitting struggle and seeking out God's truth are all possible when this takes place.

Challenge: Ask God to lead you to others who have a similar desire for righteousness. Lust thrives in the darkness. Exposing it to light deflates much of its power. You can receive help and help others if you reach out and connect within the Body of Christ for accountability partners.

_____
_____
_____
_____
_____
_____
_____
_____
_____
_____
_____
_____
_____
_____
_____
_____
_____
_____
_____
_____
_____
_____
_____
_____
_____
_____
_____
_____
_____

CHAPTER 12 - ACCOUNTABILITY

Accountable to Others

Another motivator God has given us to keep us from relapse is the threat of potential disgrace or shame before other people (Luke 14:9; Romans 1:24-26; 6:21; 1 Corinthians 11:6,14; 14:35).

We ought to be aware of how our sins impact other people and our relationships. Paul's term for this is "walking properly" (Romans 13:13; 1 Corinthians 14:40; 1 Thessalonians 4:12).

It means living in a manner of decency, and having the awareness that our actions impact those around us. We do not sin in a vacuum. Our sin impacts our families, friends, and family. Thus, it impacts our place in those relationships.

Hebrews 10:23-25 - Meet Together and Encourage Each Other - Let us hold fast the confession of our hope without wavering, for he who promised is faithful. And let us consider how to stir up one another to love and good works, not neglecting to meet together, as is the habit of some, but encouraging one another, and all the more as you see the Day drawing near.

Unchecked Lust

1. First, admit that you have a problem with lust in your life has become unmanageable.
2. Identify know where you struggle and go acknowledge it before God.
3. Safeguard yourself from people places and things.
4. Protect your family be transparent about your convictions.

We live in a world filled with lust, but that doesn't mean that we have to be consumed by it. Through the power of the Christ and the wisdom he's given us, we can conquer lust rather than be conquered by it.

Demonic strongholds of addiction can arise from ungodly bondings (or soul ties) between people. They can form with those who have had ungodly control over you. That is, through guilt, fear, or manipulation, they were able to get you to do things you would otherwise not do.

Due to our fallen nature, we will have to deal with lust until we die. The temptation to lust will come in many forms. There are external lusts, including ungodly sexual appetites and overindulgence in food and drink; and there are internal lusts, such as the lust of power, fame or position. These are major strongholds that will ultimately defeat any man or woman with uncontrolled passions. Spiritual Kryptonites (our weaknesses) can defeat us.

No matter what temptation we are faced with, our spiritual kryptonite, we can be assured that we have an Advocate who "understands every weakness of ours" and "was tempted in every way that we are. But He did not sin" (Hebrews 4:15). Jesus is not a distant God who is looking to judge you, He is your friend, and He has walked the road you are walking right now! And He has made the way of escape through Calvary .

Code of Conduct - Learning From your Failures.

Ask God for help. Sometimes we are too ashamed to take this first step. Don't try to fight the battle of lust on your own. Go to God and ask Him for help. This is what humility is all about.

Die to lust. The Bible says "sin does not have power over dead people" (Romans 6:7). So to overcome lust, we must recognize that "the persons we used to be were nailed to the cross with Jesus" (Romans 6:5). Of course, we are not actually nailed to the cross. We just recognize that our old way of life died with Jesus. When we understand what it means to be dead to sin, we will then find freedom from lust.

Walk in the Spirit. The next step is to submit your life to the Holy Spirit.

> *Galatians 5:16 - If you are guided by the Spirit, you won't obey your selfish desires.*

Remember, you can't fight lust on your own, so ask the Holy Spirit to help you.

Renew your mind. Focus on God's Word and allow Him to remove your lustful thoughts and actions (Romans 12:2). Put away everything that appeals to the flesh and focus on God (Ephesians 4:17-24; 2 Corinthians 10:5).

Resist and flee. Perhaps the best advice is simply this: Run! Don't allow lust to linger in your mind. Get far away from situations and influences that threaten to trap you (Proverbs 5:8; James 4:7-8).

My Personal Testimony

From Sin and shame to glory I have had my battles with the spirit of lust in many forms from drug addiction/pornography, highs and lows, agonies and defeat. I have come to understand through the Word of God total victory dealing with the battles of lust and sin. I am writing this book as a reminder to myself in others who have struggled.

We Are In a War

You are in a war. The enemy is attacking you now, more than you know. We are to be aware of the Devil's method of operation (2 Corinthians 2:11) so that no advantage would be taken of us by Satan for we are not ignorant of his schemes. While you may not encounter a demonic manifestation in an outward way, you are encountering them in subtle ways that can be even more devastating.

The quickest way to become a slave to sin is to practice something that is habit forming and destructive. Over eating, gambling, sex, pornography, television, social media, video games, and even prescription medication will put you on a roller coaster ride of destructive behavior. We do it to ourselves. They are self-inflicted wounds, a by-product of SIN.

Solomon says it best:

Proverbs 25:28 - A city broken into [and] left without a wall, [so] is a person who lacks self-control.

I can vaguely remember in different detail an episode of my early life where my problems began. In the writing of this book, I believe it's important to get to the point and get to the root of the problem of my roller coaster experience with sin, substance-abuse, pornography, and isolation in the terror of a sinful nature which was like a metastatic cancer that spread into my adulthood.

My addiction started at the very young of age 12 while as I was looking for acceptance and trying to find myself. I wanted to fit in with others and was not too much focused on school. It only fueled the retrogress into the areas of entrapment with sin. I begin taking on sinful traits. At that age I was very interested in girls, but I could not express myself as my brothers and uncles. I was shy, always wanting to talk and wanting to share, but not being able to effectively. There was another addiction that lurked behind my eye gates and when I opened them, satan brought in Lust. I remember a time in my neighborhood when I was still very young. Some very promiscuous sisters stripped off my clothes. I was still a virgin so this made me very uncomfortable. I was completely unsure of what to do or how to act. It wasn't long after when I stumbled across one of my step-father's pornographic books. It started an addiction and a personal stronghold that Satan used to destroy all my healthy relationships. It added to my isolated shame, so now, not only did I have an alcohol problem, but I could not communicate, I did not know how to talk to girls (I only wanted to have sex with them), and I did not even understand the basics to any kind of relationship. I forfeited every base and jumped right into sex with any girl that came around me. I was overpowered by the stronghold of lust. My addiction didn't start the first time I drink alcohol or indulged in drugs or even when I first started having sex, it all stem from the root of Sin.

The list of these things could be endless, but a few are: Our addictions, cocaine, methamphetamine, pornography, cigarettes, works of the flesh, sin to the body, things entering our eye gates, the lust of the flesh, and the lust of the eye are the pride of life. These things will disqualify anyone. ALL have sinned and come short of the glory.

Lay Aside All Sins

From my book Finish Strong:
As an author l encourages my readers to get rid of "besetting sins". This refers to sins which cling to, distract, entangle, and trip up the Christian runner. The picture is of a man trying to run a race while dressed in the long flowing robes of the day. It would be easy for him to be tripped up and fall out of the race. The Bible tells us not to be entangled with the yoke of bondage.

There are many sins that could be mentioned at this point, but the idea in this verse is that particular sin which trips you up. You know where you are weak you know your spiritual kryptonite. There are sins that do not tempt you at all, but there are others that are a constant source of temptation. This is what the writer is referring to here. Whatever that sin is, it must be stripped off and avoided at all costs. Else, it will entangle you, trip you and prevent you from finishing your race!

We Win the Battle in Jesus Christ.

There is a battle being fought and it is for soul survival. He uses the same metaphor of warfare to drive home the nature of the Christian life in 2 Timothy 2:4. Peter is equally strong when he wrote the following words in 1 Peter 2:11.

2 Peter 2:11 - Beloved, I urge you as aliens and strangers to abstain from fleshly lusts which wage war against the soul.

Although the battle is temporal (since it will end in heaven), it is persistent in time. Sin working in me is dead earnest against me. No one can turn a deaf ear to it. Every child of God is faced with this determined foe. To meet it with rules and regulations is to play according to its system. The issue is not whether the battle exists. Its presence is indisputable and non-negotiable. The issue is with what will you fight? If you lean on the arm of flesh, you will fail. But if you meet sin with grace, you have won.

Renewed Vision

After Superman discovered his weakness with kryptonite he was able to use His 'heat vision' (which was originally a by-product of the x-ray vision). The 'vision' is portrayed as either lasers shooting from his eyes, fiery optic blasts, or the literal balls of fire which they seem fond of in Smallville. The comics later explain that he's able to shoot his stored-up solar energy out through his eyes.

Spiritual Vision - Insights from Psalm 73

Truly God is good to Israel, even to such as are of a clean heart.

But as for me, my feet were almost gone; my steps had well nigh slipped.

For I was envious at the foolish, when I saw the prosperity of the wicked.

For there are no bands in their death: but their
strength is firm. They are not in trouble as other men;
neither are they plagued like other men.

Therefore pride compasseth them about as a chain;
violence covereth them as a garment.

Their eyes stand out with fatness: they have more than
heart could wish.

They are corrupt, and speak
wickedly concerning oppression: they speak loftily.

They set their mouth against the heavens, and their
tongue walketh through the earth.

Therefore his people return hither: and waters of a
full cup are wrung out to them. And they say, How
doth God know? and is there knowledge in the most
High?

Behold, these are the ungodly, who prosper in the
world; they increase in riches. Verily I have cleansed
my heart invain, and washed my hands in innocency.

For all the day long have I been plagued, and chastened
every morning.

If I say, I will speak thus; behold, I should
offend against the generation of thy children.

When I thought to know this, it was too painful for
me; Until I went into the sanctuary of
God; then understood their end.

Surely thou didst set them in slippery places: thou
castedst them down into destruction.

How are they brought into desolation, as in a moment!
they are utterly consumed with terrors.

As a dream when one awaketh; so, O Lord, when thou awakest, thou shalt despise their image.

Thus my heart was grieved, and I was pricked in my reins. So foolish was I, and ignorant: I was as a beast before thee.

Nevertheless I am continually with thee: thou hast holden me by my right hand.

Thou shalt guide me with thy counsel, and afterward receive me to glory.

Whom have I in heaven but thee? and there is none upon earth that I desire beside thee.

My flesh and my heart faileth: but God is the strength of my heart, and my portion forever.

For, lo, they that are far from thee shall perish: thou hast destroyed all them that go a whoring from thee. But it is good for me to draw near to God: I have put my trust in the Lord GOD, that I may declare all thy works.

Decree and Declare

"I break every stronghold that will take me further away from the spirit of God."

"I decree that God will show me what proper love is in the name of Jesus."

"I cancel the assignment of any demon trying to release sexual perversion on me and my family."

"I will not allow this spirit to undermine and distorts my moral and spiritual judgment."

"Father God I cancel the war between spirit and flesh and I cover myself with the blood of Jesus."

"I declare that I will not fall under the spirit of adultery in the name of Jesus."

"Your word tells me to abstain from fornication."

"I will no longer go against God's moral laws."

"God, I know that I am sanctified and set free."

"I will not allow any demon to tell me that pornography is innocent fun."

"No longer will I be a slave to any demonic forces in Jesus' name."

"I will not allow satan to whisper satanic thoughts into my mind."

"I will not believe the lies from the pits of hell."

"I declare that I will operate with the mind of Christ, every perverted desire and thought is cast down in the name of Jesus. Father God cleanse me with your blood."

"I break every stronghold that will take me further away from the spirit of God."

"I stop any unclean spirit from influencing my generation and generations to come in the name of Jesus."

"Satan the blood of Jesus is against you."

"I declare that my spiritual and natural gifts have not been violated or contaminated by any unclean spirits."

"I will not be blind by any unclean spiritual kryptonite."

"No unclean spirit will twist or pervert my thinking in the name of Jesus."

"I'm free from every ungodly soul tie that had me bound."

"I'm free from the grips of the enemy."

"I'm free of my past and present mistakes."

"My mind is free in Christ."

"I free from a low self-esteem."

"I'm free from depression and oppression in Jesus name."

"I free from the bondage of mankind."

"I'm free from every demonic trap."

"I'm free of every spoken curse spoken about me."

"I'm free from the snare of the enemy."

"I'm free from the spirit of lust."

"I'm free from bad memories."

"I'm free of the hurt from the past."

"I'm free of my guilt from my past."

"I'm free from other people's opinion."

"I'm free from a demonic mind set."

"I'm free indeed."

"I'm free from drugs"

"I release a spirit of holiness, forgiveness of self, deliverance, and the fruits of the spirit over my life in Jesus' name."

"Father, I break every vexation spirit that has come to torment me in Jesus' name."

"I will no longer allow demons to constantly harass me in Jesus' name."

"I will not give up or give in to the spirit of lust."

"My heart is fully submitted to God."

"I have been drawn away from my own lusts."

"Father God, I ask that you fully deliver me from this sexual sin."

"I am set me free from any and all evil spirits that have attached themselves to me."

The Effects of Sin

Sin offends God and always hurts the person sinning as well as our families. To choose with full knowledge and complete consent something gravely contrary to the divine law is to commit a mortal sin, which "destroys" that which the power of God has been invested in. Sin ruptures a person's relationship with God and puts his or her salvation at risk. Forgiveness is needed whenever we sin, and it is always available through our confession to Jesus Christ. Jesus over and over demonstrated his great mercy to sinners, not condemning them but saying, "Go and sin no more" (see John 8:1-11). However, persisting in sin can make it more difficult to hear God's call and respond to his offer of mercy, especially if addiction is involved.

Now, I realize that to overcome lust is a difficult task. It can be a long process, and all the more if there is an addiction. It takes time to purify our hearts and to change our mindsets. This is why we must be strong, pray like our life depended on it, fight daily against the enemy, and work toward complete freedom. Like any normal man, we are tempted many times a day with all the immodesty in our world by people, places, and things. Yet, we are called to fight against it and to find freedom, but HOW?

Only through the Word of God.

BREAKOUT SESSION

Spiritual Weapons Against Lust

Properly Directing Our Thoughts

Philippians 4:4-9 - Rejoice in the Lord always. Again I will say, rejoice! Let your gentleness be known to all men. The Lord is at hand. Be anxious for nothing, but in everything by prayer and supplication, with thanksgiving, let your requests be made known to God; and the peace of God, which surpasses all understanding, will guard your hearts and minds through Christ Jesus. Finally, brethren, whatever things are true, whatever things are noble, whatever things are just, whatever things are pure, whatever things are lovely, whatever things are of good report, if there is any virtue and if there is anything praiseworthy – meditate on these things. The things, which you learned and received and heard and saw in me, these do, and the God of peace will be with you.

Cleaning up what we messed up.

Our thoughts and desires are cleaned up gradually as we diligently resist temptation to allow adultery in our hearts — knowing that this is where evil thoughts and misdirected desires led us in the past to be overtaken by the spiritual kryptonites.

We must consciously and diligently fill the void that is left — from having abandoned lust — with that which will nourish and strengthen us by the word of God. We must fill our mind, body and soul and our spiritual house with the spiritual Power of the Word of God.

Meditating on God's Word

Psalm 119:11 - Your word I have hidden in my heart, that I might not sin against You.

In overcoming lust and learning to abide in Christ, I have found that meditating on God's Word stands out as the most powerful and enduring weapon. In fact, memorizing Scripture and bringing it to mind throughout the day has become an automatic transforming practice.

Having made God's Word my default meditation, I find that it holds me captive in a way comparable to how lust did at one time. Instead of using my imagination and inner thoughts to sin, they are being turned over to actively consider

the "unsearchable judgments" of God.
(Romans 11:33).

Hebrews 4:12 - "The Word of God is living and powerful and sharper than any two edged sword".

This effective and refined weapon honed by the Spirit and imparted through His faithful saints will succeed beyond a shadow of doubt to do its work in us if we become deeply involved ourselves in it so we don't relapse.

Persisting in Godliness

Philippians 3:12-14 - Not that I have already attained, or am already perfected; but I press on, that I may lay hold of that for which Christ Jesus has also laid hold of me. Brethren, I do not count myself to have apprehended; but one thing I do, forgetting those things which are behind and reaching forward to those things which are ahead, I press toward the goal for the prize of the upward call of God in Christ Jesus.

Galatians 6:8-9 - For he who sows to his flesh will of the flesh reap corruption, but he who sows to the Spirit will of the Spirit reap everlasting life. And let us not grow weary while doing good, for in due season we shall reap if we do not lose heart.

1 Timothy 6:7 - Persistence and consistency in maintaining our walk in the Spirit is a necessary component of our warfare against destructive sin. Throughout the history of the Church there have been those who have claimed a level of victory over the addiction of sexual lust and then "strayed from the faith".

This must not happen to us.

As we grow in recovery, we must never drop our guard or allow the sin that loaded us down so heavily in the past to again establish a foothold. The practices of our past. Each feeds off of the other. The Kryptonites need to be defeated and uprooted. This allows a harvest of good fruit to grow up. We will either become "slaves of righteousness for holiness" or slip into bondage to habitual sin of one sort or another (Romans 6:19).

Becoming a slave to righteousness is a full-time, unfinished business. It is how maturing in the faith plays out in the life of every faithful follower of Christ. If instead we become a slave to sin, there is no quick solution or effortless formula that will cause us to reverse course. It will require diligent use of the weapons described here to turn us into slaves of righteousness.

The Victory that Overcomes

"This is the victory that overcomes the world, even our faith" (1 John 4:5).

Without placing our trust in God the weapons described the Break sessions of list in conclusions of will not gain victory.

Trusting in God — biblical faith — is the shield that protects us from all attacks of the enemy. We trust Him who empowers us and is transforming us.

This balance of what we are to do versus what God does is captured clearly by Paul, when he wrote, "To this end I also labor, striving according to His working which works in me mightily" (Colossians 1:29). As Paul worked hard, so should we, in unison with God working mightily in us.

The tragedy among some Christians is that we fail to work hard when we are overwhelmed by sin. "Let go and let God" will not work if that means setting aside specific teaching of what we are to do when we fall into sin.

Entering into a consistent, biblically mandated approach to overcoming lust opens the door for God to work. Only God can change us but He does not force His way on us. Self-improvement efforts and resolution apart from surrendering to Him and His working in us is hopeless. Only He purifies the heart, filling it with His presence and love where once we were filled with sin. It is God who transforms us, not we ourselves.

As we step out in obedience we learn that our calling and His will for us goes far beyond merely removing our sin. He intends to change us.

Challenge: The weapons described here are effective means for overcoming lust in our life. Initially, the battle may be on going with agony and defeat. Be encouraged. Trust fully in God. Look to that time when victory can be rightfully claimed and celebrate recovery and live life to the fullest.

I wouldn't be who I am today without Jesus and the only thing that is keeping me is my faith in Jesus.

Forget the Past

Philippians 3:13-14 - No, dear brothers and sisters, I am still not all I should be, but I am focusing all my energies on this one thing: Forgetting the past and looking forward to what lies ahead, I strain to reach the end of the race and receive the prize for which God, through Christ Jesus, is calling us up to heaven. It is my prayer that this book be a reminder to us who have struggled with for the lust this is our weapon to go back and study and teach but most importantly live life celebrating recovery in Jesus name.

21 DAY SPIRITUAL DETOX

1. Do Not Be Deceived - 1 Corinthians 6:9-10
2. God Can Sanctify – 1 Corinthians 6:11
3. Overcome Through the Holy Spirit – Galatians 5:16-18
4. Walk in the Light – Ephesians 5:3-17
5. Set Free By His Power – John 8:31-36
6. Purify Yourself – 2 Corinthians 7:1
7. Change – Romans 15-23
8. Warning Before Destruction – 2 Peter 2:4-10 & Jude 6-7
9. Control Yourself in the Midst of Temptation – 1 Thessalonians 4:3-6 & Genesis 3:1-4
10. Resist – 1 Peter 5:8-9
11. Watch Out for the Masquerade – 2 Corinthians 11:14
12. Enticement – Proverbs 1:10
13. What's Your Desire? – James 1:13-15
14. Submit Yourself – James 4:7
15. Use the Word of God – Matthew 4:4, 7, 10
16. Pray – Matthew 6:13 & Matthew 26:41
17. Take Heed – 1 Corinthians 10:12
18. Put On The Armor of God – Ephesians 6:10-18
19. Don't Commit the Act – Genesis 39:6-20
20. Refuse to be Used – Genesis 39:9-10
21. Stay Motivated – Romans 13:13-14

Nobody will ever be perfect or attain sinlessness while still on this earth, yet it is still a goal for which we strive. The Bible makes a very strong statement regarding this in

1 Thessalonians 4:7-8, "God has called us to be holy, not to live impure lives. Anyone who refuses to live by these rules is not disobeying human rules but is rejecting God, who gives his Holy Spirit to you."

If lust has not yet gripped your heart and mind, ready yourself through a life lived above reproach to combat the temptations of lust. If you currently struggle with lust, it is time to come clean before God and ask for His intervention in your life, so that holiness can be a mark of your life as well.

It's time to make holiness Popular.

In the line of fire:

- Accept that there is a problem of addiction.

- Hate lustful habits in all forms.

- Set time frames to monitor your progress.

- Make small notes in a journal to remind yourself of the battle.

- Read motivational books.

- Join support groups.

- Be humble and don't let your ego stand in the way.

- Seek Godly counsel.

- Release the past.

- Set spiritual and physical goals.

- Let prayers and scriptures uplift your spirit

Spiritual Recall - We Are in a State of Emergency.

Act 3:19 - Repent ye therefore, and be converted, that your sins may be blotted out, when the times of refreshing shall come from the presence of the Lord

Samsung Galaxy Note7 - Recall Information

While Samsung conducts investigations of reported issues, Verizon is halting all sales of the new Note7 and exchanges for replacement Note7 devices. Customers can still bring their recalled or the new replacement Note7 devices, along with accessories they purchased from Verizon, to a Verizon corporate store for a full-refund and choose from any available devices.

- Defective Cell Phones

- Defective Cars

- Defective Christians

This defect has been identified as "Subsequential Internal Non-morality," more commonly known as S.I.N., as it is primarily expressed.

Some of the symptoms include:

1. Loss of direction

2. Foul vocal emissions

3. Amnesia

4. Lack of peace and joy

5. Selfish or violent behavior

6. Depression or confusion

7. Fearfulness

8. Idolatry

9. Rebellion

STUDY NOTES – Malachi Chapter 1

REPAIRING THE ALTAR OF THE LORD

Study Text: 1Kings 18:30-46

1. Instant answer to your prayer Psalm 50:14 - 15

❖ When you have repaired His altar, when your obedience to all His laws is complete, He said you call on me in the day of trouble and I will answer you.

2. When you have repaired the altar of God and built a new one, then your offering shall be accepted of the Lord.

❖ In Genesis 4:3 -5 two people brought offerings to God; Cain and Abel. God accepted the offering of one and rejected the offering of another.

3. When you have repaired the altar of the Lord and built a new one, then your potentials shall be activated.

❖ When the fire fell on Mount Carmel, it was an answer to prayer. Inside you is a potential, there is something God put in you when He created you, God didn't send you into this world to just come and eat and wear some dress, He wanted you to become a blessings to your generation and that will begin as you repair the altar of the Lord.

4. When you have repaired the altar of the Lord and you built a new one to him, hardship will come to an end in your life.

❖ When the fire fell on mount Carmel, it was not only the fire wood that he consumes, it consumes the rock; the symbol of hardship was removed.

➢ We need to make holiness popular again

➢ Many ignore Gods "recall notice"

➢ We need to check our Oil

▪ Conventional oil

- Conventional motor oil is a lubricant that is derived directly from crude oil. It has excellent properties that allow it to provide lubrication at high temperatures, as well as maintaining its stability over long periods of time.

  - Synthetic Oil

    - Synthetic oil is a lubricant consisting of chemical compounds that are artificially made.

Indicator Lights are On – Check Engine Lights – Change Oil Soon – Service Tire Monitor and System

➤ We need to pick up the spirit of our Pastor's Mantal

➤ We need activation.

➤ We need impartation.

➤ We need the power of God evident in our local churches, in our solemn assemblies.

➤ The church need to return back to the place of outreach/compassion.

➤ The church is having quality control issues.

➤ Appointed /Reconfirm

Acts 14:22 - Confirming the souls of the disciples, and exhorting them to continue in the faith, and that we must through much tribulation enter into the kingdom of God.

➤ Spiritual & Physical Restoration (Isaiah 53:5; 1 Peter 2:24)

Isaiah 53:5 - But he was wounded for our transgressions, he was bruised for our iniquities: the

chastisement of our peace was upon him; and with his stripes we are healed.

There is getting ready to be an exchange – A FULL REFUND!

1Thessalonians 4:4 - That every one of you should know how to possess his vessel in sanctification and honour

We must become Worshippers.

We must answer the recall Notice.

The Manufacturer, who is neither liable nor at fault for this defect, is providing factory-authorized repair and service free of charge to correct this defect.

WARNING: Continuing to operate the human being unit without correction voids any manufacturer warranties, exposing the unit to dangers and problems too numerous to list, and will result in the human unit being permanently impounded.

For free emergency service, call on God.

In politics, gridlock or deadlock or political stalemate refers to a situation when there is difficulty passing laws that satisfy the needs of the people. Gridlock can occur when two legislative houses, or the executive branch and the legislature are controlled by different political parties, or otherwise cannot agree. We are in a world plagued with one crisis after another – incurable epidemics, economic disasters, international aggression, terrorist extremism … to list only a few – what are the biggest issues facing American Christians today?

_____

_____

_____
_____
_____
_____
_____
_____
_____
_____
_____

1. Diluted faith

2. Pride

3. Bible Illiteracy

4. Closed Mind

5. No Direction on Which Way to Go

6. We Can Become the Church Laosdicea

   - pla teau A state of little or no change following a period of activity or progress.

7. Lack of Honesty

   - Who can we trust?

8. Bad Publicity

9. Back to the Basics

10. Are You Willing to Serve?

JESUS as the Repair Tech

1 Peter 1:13-21 - Wherefore gird up the loins of your mind, be sober, and hope to the end for the grace that is to be brought unto you at the revelation of Jesus Christ;

[14] As obedient children, not fashioning yourselves according to the former lusts in your ignorance:

15 But as he which hath called you is holy, so be ye holy in all manner of conversation;

16 Because it is written, Be ye holy; for I am holy.

17 And if ye call on the Father, who without respect of persons judgeth according to every man's work, pass the time of your sojourning here in fear:

18 Forasmuch as ye know that ye were not redeemed with corruptible things, as silver and gold, from your vain conversation received by tradition from your fathers;

19 But with the precious blood of Christ, as of a lamb without blemish and without spot:

20 Who verily was foreordained before the foundation of the world, but was manifest in these last times for you,

21 Who by him do believe in God, that raised him up from the dead, and gave him glory; that your faith and hope might be in God.

WINNING GOD'S WAY

When we go through tough times, we may feel God has abandoned us. However, we must stop and think. Are we headed in the wrong direction, in a way opposite of God's Word? We have to be sure we haven't turned away from the Word. God helps us recognize when we are missing the mark. He encourages us to turn from our disobedience and stay connected to Him. This is our formula for winning in battle!

- Thanks be to God, who always leads us to victory through Jesus Christ (2 Corinthians 2:14, AMP).

    1. Christ is not Jesus' last name; it means the anointed One and His anointing.

        1. The anointing is a divine empowerment.

        2. Our victory comes through the power of God.

        3. The anointing to obtain victory and to prosper is turned on when we walk in the love of God.

- Why would God allow us to go through adversity?

    1. At times, it seems the more we pray, come to church, and read the Word, the more battles we face.

        1. During testing and trials, we tend to ask, "What am I doing wrong?"

2. It is imperative during those times that we examine our hearts.

3. We may be disobeying God's Word in some way and allowing deception to govern our lives.

4. We must pay attention to the Holy Spirit's conviction in our hearts and judge our lives of any sin.

5. When we feel conviction, it is God trying to steer us in the right direction.

2. What happens when we justify our sins instead of truly repenting (turning away from them)?

1. We open ourselves to deception and weaken any sense of conviction we have.

2. We position ourselves to repeat the same act of disobedience.

3. A Believer who is desensitized to sin begins to get his or her knowledge of right and wrong from a source other than God's Word.

4. He or she loses touch with God.

• There are three things God does to persuade a disobedient Believer to come back to Him.

1. God brings conviction. He first tries to convince the person by nudging his or her heart, letting him or her

know what he or she is doing is wrong.

2. God will bring the person a prophetic message. He will use people in his or her life to try to steer him or her onto the right path.

3. God allows hardship to take over. He steps back and allows things to happen to convince the person to repent.

- Although we are afflicted at times because of His love, it is not His preferred method of dealing with us (Psalm 119:67, 75).

    1. God prefers that we judge ourselves daily and continue to obey Him.

- Why do we go through trials?

    1. "And thou shalt remember all the way which the Lord thy God led thee these forty years in the wilderness, to humble thee, and to prove thee, to know what was in thine heart, whether thou wouldest keep his commandments, or no" (Deuteronomy 8:2).

        - God wanted the Israelites to submit themselves completely to Him. True humility is the act of submitting to His Word.

        - In the midst of pressure, do you crumble and forget His Word?

    2. Trouble makes people cry out to Him (Psalm 107:25).

3. Be taught and learn from God's Word (Psalm 119:69-75).

    ▪ We allow trials to come in our lives because we refuse God's first option.

    ▪ Acknowledge God first in all of your ways.

4. Many times, God allows us to go through trials so we will know He never fails us (Acts 14:22).

5. Other times, He wants us to turn back to Him (Revelations 3:19).

6. **You Have The Victory!**
   Every believer has a responsibility to protect his or her life from the influences of lust and sin. The Bible teaches you to guard your heart (Prov. 4:23). God wants you to be a good custodian over your thought life and make sure that you only allow godly things to be planted in your mind.

   Whatever is planted will grow. Therefore, you must be selective as to what you allow your eyes to see and your ears to hear, because it will end up in the soil of your heart.

   Overcoming lust and perverted behavior is not an easy process. It takes diligence and consistency, which are both keys to breakthrough. However, should you miss the mark, remember these words from Micah 7:8, "Rejoice not against me, O mine enemy: when I fall, I shall arise...."

It's as simple as asking the Lord to forgive you and starting over again. Remember, you are more than a conqueror (Rom. 8:37), and you can do all things through Christ Jesus (Phil. 4:13)!

Journal your thoughts:

DELIVERANCE CHECKLIST

Deliverance Checklist
Questions to ask yourself

1.   What kind of spiritual oppression are you feeling? Are you experiencing any of the following: Depression, fear, voices, mental or physical illness, mental torment, spiritual torment, or chronic or routine low self esteem?

2.   Are you aware of any family members who experienced sudden trauma or death? Do you have any un-forgiveness toward yourself or others in your family? Has anyone in your family including yourself experienced physical or mental abuse,drugs, alcoholism, violence, molestation? Anything you want to add about your family's overall situation that concerns you?

3.   Unholy practices, have you ever been involved in any of the following: satanism, Freemason, Occult like objects including, Quinta Boards Witchcraft, curses, Torat cards of divination, fascination w/paranormal including shows or tours of ghost hunting, new age theories or practices, UFO's, horoscopes, communication with the dead (including relatives) pornography, lust, temper fits, religious objects or new age objects including crystals, dream catchers, or artifacts?

4.   Describe your relationship with your parents? Have you experienced any of the following; Violence, abuse whether physical or mental, problematic relations with any relative, do you have any un-forgiveness with family members or any on-going situation where hatred is still manifested. Does your family have a history of suicide, witchcraft, Native American or have they been in the occult?

5.   Have you had relationships outside of marriage? Any homosexual desires or relationships in the past. Any dreams or sexual encounters while sleeping? Have you ever been raped, molested, or part of sexual rituals. Have you had an abortion?

6.   Have you used marijuana, cocaine, speed, hallucinate products etc., Are you currently prescribed any drugs due to health concerns? Do you see things no one else sees? Do you hear voices? How often does God talk with you?

7.   Habitual Sins, do you feel that you have sin that is uncontrollable and you can not seem to stop engaging in it like; porn, anger, lust, covetous spending, hard rock, rap or unholy music, hatred, regret, past relationships unresolved, bitterness, loss of control, unexpressed guilt about your life, family or God.

8.   What is your commitment to Christ? Do you believe Christ is the virgin born Son of God, his death at the cross for your sins, and his resurrection? Would you say you trust in the finished work of Christ for your salvation? Is Jesus your Lord? If delivered would you share your testimony with others to help them find a stronger relationship with Christ?

Deliverance Questionnaire

Uncovering open doors to the demonic in a Christian's life

This questionnaire is meant to be used by a knowledgeable deliverance pastor or minister, because the reasons for each of these questions is not explained in this questionnaire. A knowledgeable deliverance minister should know the reasons behind each of these questions, and should be able to discern obvious bondages that these questions will reveal.

Each and every question does not necessarily indicate a bondage, but will help give a bigger picture to the person ministering deliverance, and can be helpful in locating obvious bondages in a person's life. These questions can reveal strongholds, demonic bondages and legal grounds that may need to be addressed.

Part I: The bondage

1. When did this bondage start?

2. Was there any unusual things that took place (or you did) when this bondage started?

3. If this bondage started when you were a child: Do you have ancestors who have suffered from a similar kind of bondage?

4. What kind of bondage are you facing? (Fears, depression, voices in your mind, mental illness, physical illness, mental torment, spiritual torment, etc.. Please be as detailed as possible.)

5. What are all the things that have impacted your life? (Parent's death, trauma, a certain situation that changed your life, anything that 'changed' you.)

Part II: Your ancestor's background

1. Do you have ancestors who have struggled with similar problems or bondages?

2. Did your bondage start as a child and appear to have no reason to be there?

3. Do you have siblings who suffer from similar bondages or oppression?

Part III: Soul ties

1. Have you been involved with extramarital sex? Are you attracted to an ex-lover? Is he or she a good/godly influence for you?

2. Have you been divorced?

3. Do you feel an unusual attraction to a past boyfriend, girlfriend or lover (who is obviously not right for you)?

4. Do you let anybody dominate, control, or make your choices you?

5. Have you ever formed a blood covenant with another person? (Blood brothers, etc.)

6. Have you ever made vows or agreements with somebody in effort to strengthen the relationship or commit yourself to each other?

7. Do you see any ungodly relationships in your past where gifts were exchanged? (Are you holding onto something that was given to you from somebody you had an adultery with, etc.)

8. Have you ever had ungodly relations with an animal?

9. Do you have any pictures in your possession of somebody whom you may have an ungodly soul tie with? (A picture of you with somebody you had an adultery with, etc.)

Part IV: Relationship with parents

1. What do you think of your parents?

2. How would you explain your childhood?

3. Where you close to your parents while growing up? If not, why?

4. How would you explain your relationship with your parents? Was it good, bad or very cold?

5. Did you feel rejection from your parents?

6. Was either of your parents overly passive or controlling?

7. Has either of your parents been divorced? Remarried? Are your parents divorced?

8. How would you describe your relationship with your siblings growing up?

Part V: Rejection and abuse

1. Were your parents married when you were conceived? Were you the right sex? Did your parents not want you, or want you to be different (gender, etc.) in any way? If so, explain.

2. Did you feel rejected as a child? As an adult? If so, by whom? Explain.

3. Did you face abuse? What kind (emotional, physical, sexual, etc.) and by whom?

4. Have you faced rejection from your peers, classmates, friends or those around you?

5. Have you ever been put down, belittled, or made fun of? If so, by whom? Explain.

6. If you have faced rejection or abuse, how did you respond? Do you feel you are still paying a price for it? If so, how?

7. How do you respond to rejection right now?

8. Do you reject yourself (self-rejection)? If so, why and in what ways?

Part VI: Unforgiveness or bitterness

1. Is there anybody you feel edgy around? (Don't like them, feel anything in your heart against them, etc.)

2. Do you have anything against anybody? In other words, is there anybody that you have a hard time demonstrating the love of Christ to?

3. Has anybody wronged you that you haven't forgiven from your heart (thoughts, feelings, emotions, etc.)?

4. How do your view your siblings, parents, coworkers, etc.? Do you have any hard feelings against them?

5. Do you make a habit of blaming yourself for everything? Do you obsess over your mistakes and feel unusually guilty for them?

6. Do you deeply regret things that you've done in your past? Could you kick yourself over something you've done in your past? If so, explain.

Part VII: Personality

1. Are you a very positive or negative person?

2. Do you feel confident in yourself? If so, why?

3. Do you have a low self esteem? If so, why?

4. Are you domineering or controlling? If so, to whom, and in what ways? Why?

5. Are you an achiever? (A go-getter) If so, in what ways?

6. Do you feel that you are always right and that if everybody did everything your way, this world would be a better place to live?

7. How do you treat your children? Husband? Are you controlling, passive, etc.?

8. Do you like people to 'look at you' (as in receive attention)?

Part VIII: Emotional health

1. Do you strive to feel accepted? If so, how does this affect your lifestyle? By whom do you want to feel accepted?

2. Are you always stressed out? If so, why?

3. Do you feel hurt? If so, by whom/what and why?

4. Do you feel good about yourself? If not, why?

5. Do you feel depressed? If so, why? When did it start? Did your parents or grandparents struggle with depression? If so, then do you know when it started and why? Do you have siblings who are also struggling? Do you feel your depression is rational or irrational?

6. Do you struggle with fears? If so, what is it that you fear? (Fear of heights, dying, being hopeless, failure, never marrying, etc.)

7. Do you worry about things? What things do you worry about? Why?

8. Do you struggle with anger? Do you have a short temper?

9. Do you have any insecurities? If so, explain.

10. Do you feel any self-pity or feel sorry for yourself? Have you ever felt this? If so, why?

11. Do you find it easy to hate people? If so, over what kinds of things would a person have to do to make you hate them?

12. Do you have any irrational feelings? If so, what are they?

13. Do you feel like something is wrong with you?

14. Do you feel excessively guilty over anything? Is this a continual problem?

15. Are you very confused and forgetful? (Beyond the normal)

16. Are you aware of any emotional wounds that have affected you?

17. Have you ever been deeply embarrassed over something? What was it?

18. Have you been in or are currently experiencing very difficult (depressing) circumstances which may cause you to feel hopeless or depressed?

Part IX: Who are you in Christ? And how do you see God?

1. How do you explain your relationship with God?

2. Do you feel you aren't good enough to meet His standards?

3. Do you see Him as a loving father, or a dictator?

4. Do you believe that it's only by the Blood of Jesus that your sins are forgiven? Or do you feel you need to earn your forgiveness in any way?

5. Do you feel God's love in your life?

6. Do you feel like your sins are forgiven? Or do you feel guilty?

7. Do you feel excessively guilty in everyday life?

8. Do you feel that doing good things, you earn God's love and acceptance?

9. Do you feel that God is angry or upset with you?

Part X: Spoken curses, vows & oaths

1. Have you ever spoken something negative about yourself that has came to past? For example: "I'm sick and tired..." or "If I don't quit typing, I'm going to get arthritis!"

2. Has your parents, or those in authority over you spoken out a curse over you? For example: "You'll never amount to anything!" or "You'll never get out of debt" or "You're so dumb"

3. Have you ever made a vow out of anger? If so, what? For example: "I'll never let anybody push me around again!" or "I'm never going to be hurt again!"

4. Have you ever wished to die? Have you ever said it?

5. If you have made any vows or oaths, what are they?

Part XI: Relationships

1. Do you have many friends? What kind of people are they?

2. Do you have a hard time trying to meet new people or make friends?

3. Are you socially outgoing or shy? If so, why?

4. How would you define your relationship with your spouse?

Part XII: Sexuality

1. Have you ever had unholy sex? What kind? (Fornication, adultery, sodomy, bestiality, with a child, etc.)

2. Have you struggled with lust, fantasy or unholy sexual thoughts? If so, what kind?

3. Have you been attracted to pornography?

4. Do you have homosexual thoughts and desires? If so, have you acted upon those feelings?

5. How do you feel about your sexuality? (Do you feel dirty about it, or do you feel it's a wonderful blessing that God's given you?)

6. Do you withhold sex from your spouse or are you fidgety? Do you enjoy a healthy relationship with your spouse sexually? How does he or she react?

7. Have you ever been raped or sexually abused?

8. Have you ever woke up and felt a sexual presence with you? There are demons that imitate male and female functions, and stimulate their host (a person) sexually (beyond the normal 'wet dream').

9. Do you struggle or have you struggled with masturbation?

10. Do you struggle or have you struggled with any other sexual related thoughts, desires, or bondages?

11. Is there anything sexually that you are ashamed of?

Part XIII: Addictions

1. Do you have any addictions? If so, what kind? (Drugs, alcohol, smoking, eating, sex, TV, etc.) When did they start?

2. Did anybody else in your family (siblings, ancestors, etc.) have a struggle with any addictions? If so, what? Who?

3. Have you ever had, or currently have any sort of obsession over anything? If so, what?

Part XIV: False religions

Examples of false religions: Buddhism, Hindu, Jehovah Witness, Mormonism, Christian Scientists, eastern religions, etc.

1. Have you ever been involved with any false religions? If so, why, when and how long? How do you feel about those beliefs now?

2. Have you ever been involved in any secret societies such as Freemasonry? If so, how deep were you involved?

Part XV: The occult & Satanism

1. Have you ever shown interest in the occult? If so, in what ways? (Read up on it, dabbled in it, etc.)

2. Do you still feel drawn or attracted to the occult?

3. Have you had any interest in horror or thriller style movies or novels? Are you still attracted to these things?

4. Have you ever made a vow with the devil? If so, what?

5. Married Satan?

6. Worshipped a demon or Satan?

7. Have you ever put a curse or spell on somebody?

8. Are you aware of any curses or spells placed on you? If so, what? Who did it?

9. Dabbled with an Ouija board? If so, why?

10. Ever been a member of a coven (group of 13 witches)? Explain.

11. Communicated with the dead? Explain.

12. Told somebody's fortune or went to see a fortune teller? Explain.

13. Ever read your horoscope?

14. Watched or been involved in a séance? Explain.

15. Been involved or a victim of Satanic Ritual Abuse (SRA)? Explain.

16. Been baptized into a false religion or any other evil baptism? If so, what were you baptized into? When?

17. Have you ever had a spirit guide?

18. Have you ever been involved with meditation, yoga, karate, or related activities?

19. Were you or anybody in your family superstitious? If so, who?

20. Ever been involved in astral travel? (Out of body)

21. If you have made any vows or oaths, what are they? Were there any sacrifices or rituals that was accompanied with them?

22. Have you ever made a blood pact before? If so, with whom (including persons, demons and Satan) and for what purpose?

23. Have you ever partaken in automatic writing, automatic drawing or automatic painting?

24. Have you ever been involved in Yoga, transcendental meditation, or similar activities?

25. Have you ever sought healing from a spiritual source other than Jesus Christ? (New age healing, energy healing, etc.)

26. Any other involvement in the occult? Explain.

Part XVI: Un-confessed sins

1. Are there any un-confessed sins that you have not repented of? (Usually something you've done, that you know is wrong, but won't admit to it. An abortion, stealing, etc. are some examples.)

2. Is there anything you've been hiding inside that you haven't confessed?

3. Do you feel excessively guilty over some thing(s) you've done in the past? If so, what?

Part XVII: Cursed objects

1. Do you have any idols, occult rings, or anything that could hold evil spiritual value in your home? If so, what? Any objects that hold evil spiritual value must be destroyed.

2. Do you have any gifts saved from sinful relationships? If so, explain. For example, if a man gives a woman a personal gift during an adultery, that needs to be sold or destroyed.

Part XVIII: Severe trauma, abuse & disassociation

1. Have you ever been exposed to extreme abuse or a traumatic experience? Did it have a drastic effect on your emotional or mental system? If so, what happen? How did it affect you?

2. Have you ever disassociated or been diagnosed with Dissociative Identity Disorder (DID) or Multiple Personality Disorder (MPD)?

3. Are you aware of any alters (other personalities) that you may have? (If so, tell me about them)

4. Do you have a memory gap where you cannot remember a certain time of your life?

5. Do you have false memories of things that really didn't take place?

6. Have you ever been in a car accident or other traumatic situation? Have you ever witnessed a tragedy in real life?

Part XIX: Weaknesses

1. Do you struggle with any habitual sins? If so, what? Do you want to break those bad habits?

2. Do you struggle with any weaknesses such as lust, anger, hate, etc.? If so, what? Do you know where they came from or how they got started? Do you want to break free from those weaknesses?

Part XX: Pregnancy issues

1. Have you ever said something along the lines of, "I will never have children"?

2. Have you ever had an abortion or attempted one?

3. Have you ever had incest or ungodly sexual relations with somebody related to you? (See Leviticus 20:19-21, as this can cause a curse to land upon you which needs to be broken)

Part XXI: Other things to look for

1. Have you ever tried drugs? If so, how much, and how did it affect you? Why did you try drugs?

2. Have you ever thought about or attempted suicide?

3. Do you have any physical or mental disabilities, diseases or illnesses? Explain.

4. Do you want, and are willing to be delivered? Are you willing to give up those demon spirits and maybe make some lifestyle changes in order to keep your deliverance?

5. Do you experience unusual confusion settle upon you as you try to pray and read the Bible?

6. What kind of music do you like? (Please list all styles of music you currently enjoy, and give examples in each category you list, such as some names of artists and songs)

7. Have you previously enjoyed hard rock, metal, acid, alternative, rap, new age, or any other kind of worldly music? (Please provide some examples of artists and songs from each genre (type/style) of music you list)

8. Have you had any nightmares or weird experiences at night while supposedly sleeping?

9. Have you ever been in a trance or had an out of body experience?

10. Have you ever noticed time slipped right out from under you? For example, you look at your watch and it's 7:00pm, then you look again what seemed like 15 minutes later and it's 2:00am. This is a sign of a trance.

11. Have you ever touched or kissed a dead body? If so, explain whom and why and what happened afterwards.

12. Do you feel that you somehow have to earn your forgiveness? Do you 'wonder' if your sins are truly forgiven -- all of them? Are you aware of any signs of legalism or religious spirits operating in your mind?

13. Do you have any physical infirmities, sickness or diseases? If so, please list them.

14. Are you on any medications? If so, please explain.

15. Are you entertained by movies or tv shows which glorify death, murder, pain or suffering of others? Please explain.

16. Have you ever had any other kind of weird encounter with the spiritual realm?

Journal your thoughts:

CONCLUSION

As we conclude, let me remind you that Superman's weakness was kryptonite. When Superman was exposed to kryptonite, it caused him to become weak, to lose his superhuman abilities, and to begin to die at a rapid pace. In order for Superman to survive, the kryptonite needed to be removed from his presence.

In the same way, when we, as Christians, entertain our own weaknesses (when we routinely allow them to take control our lives), we become weak spiritually and we begin to die at a rapid pace. When that happens, we must take immediate action. We must root those sins out; we must not make provision for the flesh; and we must submerge ourselves in service to God.

Like Superman or Superwoman, the sky is the limit for you when you Say No to Kryptonite by setting boundaries. Try putting your hand up in a stop position and yelling "No!" It's a powerful way to feel yourself setting a boundary. Or when you drive past an old favorite bar or using spot, keep your eyes straight ahead and move forward into your future instead of turning into your unhealthy past.

We have to come clean, or stay away nasty.

Finish strong, you might've done with the world say you've done but you know who the world say you are.

Be like Superman, more powerful than a locomotive when it comes to your recovery. So put that "S" on your chest; no one has to know it's there but you!

YOU HAVE SUPER POWERS!

No you can't fly and you can't see through walls or shoot spider webs out of your hands but you are equipped with super powers and trust me they are much better and longer lasting!

- We have the authority of Christ! (John 14:12, Matt 28:19-20)

- We have Superhuman Supernatural powers! (Mark 16:17, Phil 4:13)

- We have superhuman armor and weapons! (Eph 6, 2 Cor 10:5, 1 Cor chapter 12-14)

- We are not human when we yield to the powers of the Holy Spirit

- We are supernatural!

Still not convinced? (well did you read ALL the verses?) The Bible says that we can do the things that Jesus did and even greater things! What are some things Jesus did? He healed the sick, preached the good news with Authority, loved EVERYONE, raised the dead, walked on water, and MUCH, MUCH MORE!!! The Bible also says we can lay hands on the sick and they shall be healed! It says we can pick up serpents and if we drink anything deadly it will not hurt us. However, of all these powers that we have there is one that is the most important and that is the power to point people to Jesus and see them rescued from the grasps of hell. The power to change someone's life eternally. He brought me from Sin & Shame to Glory!

Superman cannot even claim that! YOU ARE A HERO. YOU HAVE POWERS.YOU MAY BE THE ONLY JESUS PEOPLE WILL EVER MEET.YOU

MAY BE THE ONLY HOPE FOR THE PEOPLE
AT YOUR WORK, SCHOOL, CHURCH, FAMILY,
TOWN, AND CITY THE NATIONS.

Journal your thoughts:

_____

_____

_____

_____

_____

_____

_____

_____

_____

_____

_____

_____

_____

_____

_____

_____

_____

_____

_____

_____

_____

_____

_____

_____

_____

_____

_____

_____

_____

_____

_____

_____

THE CHRISTIAN 12 STEPS

12 steps programs have been helping people overcome problems with addiction for nearly a century, and literally millions of people have achieved the salvation of sobriety by following these 12 honest steps of life improvement and honesty before God.

There is nothing easy about recovery from addiction, although with the assistance and love of Jesus Christ, a better life of service and happiness is always possible. All addicts who want to make a change will need to commit to an honest admission of defects, and take the steps necessary before God and man to better these faults of character, and live a happier life without the pain of substance abuse.

The Christian 12 steps movement obviously originates out of the root successes of the original 12 steps programs, but to better serve the needs of Christians in recovery, Christians have modified those 12 steps.

Praying to Jesus Christ

Praying to a higher power never made much sense to Christians in the program, and so in Christian recovery, not only do we pray to Jesus, but we also study the wisdom of the bible for strength and meaning, and we search our souls for ways we can live better lives in the image of God.

The ARRM Christian 12 steps

1. We admitted we were powerless over our addictions and dysfunctional- behaviors, that our lives had become unmanageable.
2. Came to believe that God, a Power greater than ourselves, could restore us to sanity and stability.

3. Made a decision to turn our will and our lives over to the care of God as revealed in the Bible.
4. Made a searching and fearless moral inventory of ourselves.
5. Admitted to God, to ourselves, and to another human being the exact nature of our wrongs.
6. Were entirely ready to have God remove all these defects of character.
7. Humbly asked Him to remove our shortcomings.
8. Made a list of all persons we had harmed, and became willing to make amends to them all.
9. Made direct amends to such people wherever possible, except when to do so would injure them or others.
10. Continued to take personal inventory and when we were wrong promptly admitted it.
11. Sought through prayer and meditation to improve our conscious contact with God as revealed in the Bible, praying only for knowledge of His will for us and the power to carry that out.
12. Having had a spiritual awakening as the result of these steps, we tried to carry this message to others, and to practice these principles in all our affairs.

7 Keys of Service

Connect - Join the Team

1. Senior Pastor Support/testimony vision - Our senior pastor's support makes it acceptable for someone to be in recovery.
2. Worship - Is a major difference between a Christ-centered and a secular recovery program. Worship starts off getting connected to God and others.
3. ARRM New Groups – Open Share groups are built around individual needs and recovery

issues, new groups act like blood transfusions in our recovery ministry.

4. ARRM Fellowship events- Our recovery program needs to be out in the open, a regular place where people in recovery can join together.

5. ARRM Curriculum - Learn to implement this curriculum that is built on God's Word. Step study Groups provides a group environment to work through the ARRM Recovery participant guides

6. ARRM Outreach – Recovery is an outreach opportunity to connect with the un- churched in your community.

7. Leadership training- Once you stop learning, you stop growing. Trained Mentors Leaders will keep your Recovery Healthy and growing.

#Sin&ShameToGlory #FinishStrong

Conclusion Victory Testimonies

I would love to interview you if you had any type of struggles with lust. This book will be a training manual for anybody dealing with any addiction, it is designed to train your eyes and defeat the enemy that destroy families through pornography and/or drug addiction.

Share your story with me by emailing me privately at pastorcflow@aol.com

I will keep all your information you share with me confidential. You name will not be mentioned. It will be used for the purpose of writing a follow up training manual.

Give examples of defeat in the struggle that we have as men and women with addiction in order to give our readers different scenarios of the bondage of addiction.

Thank you in advance.

Do you have something to share with me that can help somebody else?

ABOUT THE AUTHOR

Apostle Carl Flowers is passionate about deliverance Ministry and addiction recovery and gives all the glory to God for his personal deliverance.

Has been in ministry since 1995. He is an ordained Apostle and Licensed Senior Pastor through Trinity Outreach Ministries, and his vision for ministry is to provide life-changing experiences through anointed teaching and preaching of The Gospel of Christ, and by developing and sharing ways for God's people to "live out our faith" in practical yet meaningful ways in our city, our nation, and around the world.

His philosophy is simple. "True Christians follow Christ, relate honestly to God, and make a positive impact everywhere we go"! He hopes that you will come and visit us, and consider becoming a part of our growing ministry.

Our Co-Pastor, Prophetess Julie Flowers, a true Woman of God who is passionate about the true meaning of real salvation. She is a woman of God who preaches and teaches the unadulterated word of truth. Prophetess Julie, Co-Pastor, wants everyone to learn, know, and understand that Salvation is a process that ultimately leads to an Anointing of The Baptism of The Holy Spirit. She and Apostle Flowers and our entire congregation believe that "signs and wonders" are to accompany the true believers of God's Word, and that there is Peace, Purpose, and Power in living a life that is fully surrendered to The Father, The Son, and The Holy Spirit.

"For Thine is The Kingdom, The Power, and The Glory...forever. This ministry was founded on faith love and commitment. Deliverance healing and restoration has been the children's bread.

Pastor Flowers has a Bachelors degree in Biblical Studies/Biblical Counseling from Covenant Bible College & Seminary in Tallahassee Florida

He is a Author of three books:
From Sin & Shame to Glory, Finish Strong and Spiritual Kryptonite.

He is the Founder Director of "Addiction Recovery Restoration Ministry" (ARRM) which teaches weekly the divine word of deliverance through Jesus Christ.